Amsterdam to Nairobi

Amsterdam to Nairobi

The World Council of Churches and the Third World

Ernest W. Lefever

Foreword by George F. Will

Ethics and Public Policy Center
Georgetown University
Washington, D.C.

Ernest W. Lefever, the founding director of the Ethics and Public Policy Center, is also a professorial lecturer in the Department of Government at Georgetown University and a faculty associate of its Center for Strategic and International Studies. He has a B.D. and a Ph.D. in Christian ethics from Yale University. Among the books he has written are *Ethics and United States Foreign Policy* (1957), *Uncertain Mandate: Politics of the U.N. Congo Operation* (1967), *Spear and Scepter: Army, Police, and Politics in Tropical Africa* (1970), and *Nuclear Arms in the Third World: U.S. Policy Dilemma* (1979).

George F. Will is a columnist syndicated by the Washington Post Writers Group, a columnist for *Newsweek*, and a commentator on NBC's "Today" show. He has a Ph.D. in political science from Princeton University. He is the author of *The Pursuit of Happiness and Other Sobering Thoughts* (1978).

Library of Congress Cataloging in Publication Data:
Lefever, Ernest W
    Amsterdam to Nairobi.
    Includes bibliographical references.
    1. World Council of Churches.   2. Church and underdeveloped areas.   I. Georgetown University, Washington, D.C. Ethics and Public Policy Center. II. Title.
BX6.W78L43   261.8   79-2607
ISBN 0-89633-025-7
ISBN 0-89633-024-9 pbk.

Contents

Appendixes

Foreword

By George F. Will

THE WORLD COUNCIL OF CHURCHES, a politically active organization, is justly famous for both the intensity and the selectivity of its indignation. That is why it is the center of a boiling controversy. What is at issue is not "activism" versus "quietism" in Christian life. Rather, the questions are whether the WCC is an appropriate instrument for Christian action; and whether the WCC is active on behalf of decent causes; and whether the WCC is indecently quiet about indecencies committed by regimes and movements on the left.

Let us be clear, as Professor Ernest Lefever is, about what the question is not. It is not whether Christians should be politically active, or whether their faith should inform their action. Of course they should; of course it should. But over the years good Christians (meaning, in this instance, good people who have been, by their lights, conscientious in trying to fulfill their faith) have identified with a wide variety of regimes and political causes. (It is an open question whether, in particular cases, the identification reflected a flaw in their Christianity.) Christ was, to say no more, impatient with this world, and he urged only a provisional attachment to any part of it, including any regime or social system. Christians believe that the world is under judgment, including its institutions. But it is wrong to believe that this means that Christianity is somehow "inherently" revolutionary, or that Christians can casually undertake or underwrite political upheavals. Political revolutionaries almost invariably invest in politics a kind of expectation that mature Christians consider not just unrealistic but unseemly. Furthermore, even when Christianity was young, and was considered a subversive sect, its leader insisted that there were things his followers must render unto Caesar. It is well to remember that when Peter enjoined the faithful to "fear God, honor the king," the king was Nero. There is at least some scriptural basis for many sharply divergent attitudes about politics. That proves nothing; complex institutions contain contradictions.

Today, a Christian attitude that is familiar in fact and in satire is that of the Trendy Cleric who will let no "progressive" parade pass unjoined. When Prime Minister Harold Macmillan was asked if he would provide Britons with a sense of purpose, he replied, splendidly, that for a sense of purpose they should go to their archbishops. But, as has been said, the trouble is that archbishops are apt merely to send people back to politics. There is a kind of clergyman for whom theological interests are peripheral and political interests are central. Others insist that politics "really" is theology carried on by other means, means "appropriate" to the times.

The dotty curate dabbling in radicalism has become a figure of fun. But the WCC is larger than (although it is in many ways less than) a curate. It is an international organization with the mighty pretense of being at once a representative and a prophetic institution. And the WCC does more than dabble. It lends material and moral support. Sometimes what it supports is not abstract radicalism, not idle ideology, not mere pamphleteering, but armed and killing terrorism.

The WCC is not important because its activities are history-making. They are not. But the WCC is, if not especially important, at least interesting because it carries a familiar but endlessly fascinating virus. The WCC is a carrier of "liberation theology." This is a relatively recent wrinkle in an old phenomenon. That phenomenon is the suspension of critical faculties by Western intellectuals when confronted by Marxist criticisms of Western culture. Professor Peter Berger writes:

> Since the late 1960s there has been a widespread identification of Christian morality, if not Christianity as such, with the political agenda of the left. The concept of "liberation" has come to serve as the *idée-clef* of this identification. . . . There may be all sorts of *normative* assumptions underlying the new Christian leftism—about the moral imperatives of the Gospel, about human rights, about egalitarianism, and so on—but the application of these norms to concrete sociopolitical situations depends on a *cognitive* grid: "This is what the world is like."
>
> Thus we are told that capitalism is intrinsically exploitative and oppressive, that socialism by contrast is intrinsically "liberating," that America is the most violent nation on earth, that racism is endemic to Western culture, and so on. These and comparable statements are not primarily normative; rather, they purport to be statements of facts. . . . And the most important criticism to be made of the new Christian leftism is *not* that it promulgates false norms, *nor* that it is theologically mistaken, *but that it is based on demonstrable*

misconceptions of empirical reality. Put differently: What is most wrong about "liberation theology" is neither its biblical exegesis nor its ethics but its sociology.*

Professor Berger is, I think, carrying Christian charity too far. Criticism of the ethics of this leftism is at least as warranted as is criticism of its sociology. But readers of Professor Lefever's essay can decide for themselves the extent to which bad sociology, bad theology, bad faith, and, yes, sin feed on one another and are to blame for what the WCC has been doing. The thoroughly modern reader may find the idea of sinfulness quaint; but few readers will believe that the WCC is not blameworthy.

This has been a bloody century not only because, as Yeats said, "the worst are full of passionate intensity," but also because some of the well-intentioned have been so useful to the worst. The record of the WCC is only in part a record of some people who are well-intentioned but breathtakingly silly. Some of the people involved are more sinister than silly, and even those who are "only" silly are culpable. Always, but especially in the high-stakes business of politics, there is a moral obligation to be intelligent.

*Peter Berger and others, "A Politicized Christ" (a discussion of *Christianity and the World Order* by Edward Norman), in *Christianity and Crisis,* March 19, 1979.

Preface

"WHILE SAINTS ARE ENGAGED in introspection, burly sinners run the world," said John Dewey. The leaders of the World Council of Churches, the foremost manifestation of the ecumenical movement, have never accepted this division of labor. And they are right. Throughout the history of Christianity its saints and sinners have insisted that the church and individual Christians should have some responsibility for the quality of the social, economic, and political order. But they have disagreed on what this responsibility is and how it should be expressed.

Today the World Council of Churches is the eye of a swirling controversy about this fundamental question. The Roman Catholic Church and all other major religious traditions also continue to wrestle over the proper relation between the City of God and the City of Man.

Yet most Christians believe that somehow religion should be the conscience of society, and many of them would accept the judgment of William Temple, the late Archbishop of Canterbury and a pioneer ecumenical leader, who in 1942 said: "Nine-tenths of the work of the Church in the world is done by Christian people fulfilling responsibilities and performing tasks which are not part of the official system of the Church at all." He cited the abolition of the slave trade as an example. A man of compassion and worldly wisdom, Temple defined government as "the art of so ordering life that self-interest prompts what justice demands."

I have written this essay on the World Council and the Third World as a participant in and observer of the ecumenical movement and as one who affirms the hope of Christian unity. I also believe that the churches have an obligation to seek greater justice, freedom, and security in this world. Between my B.D. and Ph.D. studies, both in Christian ethics at Yale University, I spent three years with the War Prisoners' Aid of the World's YMCA in Britain and West Germany (1945-48). Later I was the associate director for international affairs of the U.S. National Council of Churches

(1952-54). I attended the Amsterdam Assembly (1948) and the Evanston Assembly (1954) of the World Council of Churches. Professional activities have taken me to some sixty Third World countries on three continents. Recently my latest book, *Nuclear Arms in the Third World: U.S. Policy Dilemma*, was published by the Brookings Institution.

The present study is a survey and a critique of the activities the World Council has undertaken to meet the needs and aspirations of peoples in Asia, Africa, and Latin America. It is intended to stimulate informed debate on the character and impact of the Council's witness in the larger political drama with a view to making its work more responsible and effective. Consequently, it focuses on the controversial actions of the Council, rather than on its nonpartisan relief and welfare activities in the Third World. In my view the current debate has suffered because some of the more uncomfortable questions have not been adequately aired. In raising these questions, I have been encouraged by the words of the French theologian Georges Bernanos: "The worst, the most corrupting lies are problems poorly stated." The "right" questions do not necessarily lead to the "right" answers, but they do facilitate candid discourse.

Official World Council pronouncements are quoted frequently throughout the text. To give a fuller picture of the Council's views, I have included in the appendixes generous selections from the reports of the Amsterdam Assembly (Appendix A) and the Nairobi Assembly in 1975 (Appendix B), as well as four documents on the Council's Program to Combat Racism: a tabulation of grants 1970-78 (Appendix F), two official explanations (Appendixes E and G), and a recent statement of the Council's Central Committee supporting the program (Appendix I).

I acknowledge with pleasure the valuable aid and advice I received over the past three years in the preparation of this study. I owe a special debt to Elliott Wright and Kenneth Adelman for writing extensive background analyses. Three Georgetown University students, Matthew G. Maloney, David R. Rivero, and Gary Hayes, provided research assistance.

The study has also benefited from the critical comments of Paul Bock, Martin F. Herz, Patricia McGrath, J. Robert Nelson, Richard John Neuhaus, and Paul G. Schrotenboer. The editing was done by Carol Griffith.

As with all Center publications, the author alone is responsible for the selection of facts and for the views expressed.

ERNEST W. LEFEVER, *Director*
Ethics and Public Policy Center

July 1979

CHAPTER ONE

How the Churches Speak to the World

The Spirit of the Lord is upon me, because he has anointed me to preach good news to the poor. He has sent me to proclaim release to the captives and recovering of sight to the blind, to set at liberty those who are oppressed. . . .

LUKE 4:18 (QUOTING ISAIAH 61:1)

ON AUGUST 10, 1978, World Council of Churches officers announced a grant of $85,000 to the Patriotic Front guerrillas who by violence were seeking to overthrow the interracial interim regime in Rhodesia. The money, given by the Council's Special Fund to Combat Racism, was to be used by the guerrillas for food, health, agriculture, refugee aid, and other humanitarian purposes. But the Council made no provision for any independent agency to see how the funds were spent.

The grant was widely criticized in religious and secular circles because it lent material aid and political support to Cuban-trained, Soviet-equipped, and Marxist-oriented forces. Like most military efforts that employ terrorist tactics, the Front, operating from bases in Mozambique and Zambia, deliberately selected innocent civilians for murder and kidnapping. Its goal since March 1978 was to replace the four-man executive council in Rhodesia, made up of Prime Minister Ian Smith and three black nationalist leaders. Together two of the nationalists, Methodist bishop Abel Muzorewa and Congregationalist minister Ndabaningi Sithole, were widely believed to command majority political support throughout the country. The WCC gave Muzorewa and Sithole $110,000 in 1975 and 1976 but declined to make further grants to them after they joined with Smith in the interim regime, which was seeking to establish by peaceful and constitutional

1

means, including a universal adult franchise, a democratic, multi-party government that would guarantee civil and political rights to all racial groups in the new Rhodesia-Zimbabwe. The constitution endorsed by the four men provided for twenty-eight white seats in a parliament of one hundred to ensure continuity and prevent white flight, which had had disastrous economic and political consequences in a dozen or more other black African states.

At the time the WCC grant was announced, one-man–one-vote elections were scheduled in Rhodesia for December 1978, but they were postponed because of the guerrilla assaults and other external circumstances. The elections were held in April 1979 in full view of several hundred observers from abroad, who had complete freedom of movement in the country. Of the 2.9 million eligible black voters, 64.4 per cent cast their ballots in the face of threats of death from the Front guerrillas and a number of well-publicized attacks on polling places in rural areas. This contrasts with a 35 per cent turnout in the 1978 U.S. congressional election. The voters, black and white, had a choice of five black-led parties. Bishop Muzorewa's United African National Council won 67 per cent of the votes, and he became the first prime minister of Rhodesia-Zimbabwe. Trained observers sent by New York–based Freedom House concluded that the election was conducted fairly, was a "significant advance toward majority rule," and was more free than "elections in most developing countries."[1]

Shortly before the 1978 WCC grant, the guerrillas had deliberately killed thirty-five foreign missionaries and their children in Rhodesia. Not long thereafter they had shot down an unarmed civilian plane and murdered all of the survivors. The top black leaders in the country and their lieutenants had been tagged for assassination, and several of Mr. Sithole's associates had already been killed.

Throughout the United States and Europe, church leaders, the press, and others condemned the grant as an irresponsible manifestation of Christian charity. It provoked an "enormous disturbance" in British churches, according to one WCC Executive Committee member, and in West Germany a top churchman reported "bitter reaction" among churches long associated with the Council.[2] A United Presbyterian layman, noting that three of the outside parties supporting the Rhodesian guerrillas were the Soviet Union, Cuba, and the World Council of Churches, concluded that the "apologists" for the WCC grant had an ideological preference for Marxism over Christianity.[3] In more moderate tones, the Inter-Church

Relations Board of the Presbyterian Church in Ireland pleaded for "caution and restraint" and said, "Grants made by well-intentioned donors to paramilitary or guerrilla groups . . . do not end simply with humanitarian aid, . . . but strengthen generally the power" of the group being assisted.[4] (See Appendix H.)

WCC officials dismissed the criticism as invalid. Council spokesman Bruno Kroker reportedly said the outrage against the grant stemmed mainly from "misinformation" spread by "hate-mongering journalists."[5] As if to show it was determined to pursue its chosen course, the WCC, a month after the $85,000 grant, announced a $125,000 contribution to SWAPO, the South West Africa People's Organization. This Marxist-oriented guerrilla force was attempting to prevent the peaceful transition of South West Africa (Namibia) to an independent, democratic state under an internal constitutional process based on a universal adult vote. The 1978 grant brought total WCC support for SWAPO to $498,500 (see Appendix F).

The WCC's chief vehicle for assisting "liberation" movements is its Program to Combat Racism (PCR). Since 1970 the PCR has given $3,063,545 for "humanitarian" assistance to more than a hundred organizations in some two dozen countries. Almost 65 per cent of that has gone to guerrilla groups and other organizations seeking to overthrow white regimes (and in 1978 two interim interracial regimes, in Rhodesia and South West Africa) in southern Africa, and to groups elsewhere supporting political change in that region.

The City of God and the City of Man

These two controversial WCC grants dramatize the perplexing questions Christians have always faced in attempting to relate the demands of their faith to the poverty, injustice, and lack of freedom in the larger social and political order. These problems exist in one form or another in all states—democratic, authoritarian, or totalitarian. From its beginning the church and its members have lived in two worlds, this world and the next, or what St. Augustine called "the city of man" and "the city of God." The Christian faith speaks to the total human condition—to the individual, but also to the larger world. Throughout the ages theologians and the faithful have struggled to reconcile the sometimes conflicting demands of individual conscience and social responsibility.

The great majority of Christians, past and present, believe that they as individuals and the churches as corporate bodies have a social responsibility, but they disagree sharply on the nature of that responsibility and how it should be carried out. A premise of this study is that the churches, and in a larger sense religion, serve as the conscience of society. Hence Christian bodies have an obligation to speak out against gross evils and to make their voices heard on the great moral issues. This speaking out—whether in sermons, articles, educational materials, or formal pronouncements—should be responsible. Pronouncements should emerge from an intensive dialogue that seeks to discover the implications of the Christian Gospel for the particular social or political issue addressed. This dialogue must be true to the theological and social teachings of the churches and must take into account the facts of the situation. In short, church pronouncements should be morally sound and empirically informed if they are to be politically relevant.

There is not, of course, one single Christian social tradition that can serve as a universal and absolute guide. Among the several streams of Christian thought, some emphasize the other-worldly elements of the Christian faith—personal salvation and preparation for the next world—over the concerns of this world. Of those traditions that acknowledge the necessity for a "social gospel," there are two principal schools: one stresses continuity, orderly change, and reform; the other, radical discontinuity and revolutionary change. Both schools affirm the values of justice, freedom, security, and peace, but they differ on which has priority in particular circumstances.

Christians also divide over what can be expected from human nature and what can be achieved in history. Some believe in the perfectibility of man and the possibility, if not inevitability, of progress in history. Others place a greater stress on original sin; hence they expect less from history and strive for less ambitious political and social goals. In short, a few Christians believe the Kingdom of God will be established within history, while most believe it awaits the end of history. Within the latter category, there are wide differences over the appropriate means to use in working for greater justice, freedom, and order.

It is dangerous for any Christian body to identify itself fully with any specific political cause or order, whether the prevailing one or a challenge to it. In identifying with a secular power or agency, the church runs the risk of losing its critical distance and of subverting its prophetic function, its capacity to judge all movements and systems by universal Christian standards. It is thus just as foolish, as Professor Edward Norman points out, for the church to endorse Julius Nyere's Tanzanian Christian socialism as it is to support Franco's Fascist Spain.[6] Christians can and should support justice, freedom, the rule of law, and respect for the human person.

The World Council of Churches and How It Operates

The principal objective of the World Council of Churches, and of the ecumenical movement in general, is to develop greater Christian unity among the various traditions and denominations. (The word "ecumenical" derives from the Greek *oikoumenē*, meaning "the inhabited world.") After a decade of planning, interrupted by World War II, the Council was created at the inaugural Assembly in Amsterdam in August 1948. Its member denominations at that time numbered 152 from 46 countries. Today the WCC has 295 member churches from 100 countries.

The WCC emerged from six international conferences. (A list of major ecumenical meetings appears as Appendix D.) (1) At the World Missionary Conference held in Edinburgh in 1910, European and American mission leaders discussed their task of spreading the Gospel. This led to the creation in 1921 of the International Missionary Council. (2) In 1925, Orthodox, Protestants, and Anglicans interested in applying Christian principles to world problems gathered in Stockholm. Out of this grew the Universal Christian Council on Life and Work. (3) The World Conference on Faith and Order, held in Lausanne, Switzerland, in 1927, dealt with doctrinal points dividing the various denominations. (4) In 1937, the Life and Work movement, meeting at Oxford University, and (5) the Faith and Order movement, meeting at Edinburgh, agreed on a plan of union. (The International Missionary Council remained separate until 1961.) And (6) in 1938 church representatives met at Utrecht, the Netherlands, to lay plans for the proposed World Council of Churches.

From its outset the WCC has had two main streams, reflecting the two movements brought together by its founding. *Faith and Order* has been concerned with doctrinal and ecclesiastical differences, and with promoting the Christian faith around the world. *Life and Work* has focused on the application of Christianity to social, political, and cultural problems. (Within the WCC, Life and Work later came to be called *Church and*

Society.) The two emphases continue side by side, sometimes complementing and sometimes conflicting with each other. Their interplay can be seen in the evolving responses of the World Council of Churches to the needs and problems of the Third World.

As in any large, bureaucratic organization, the decisions of the WCC emerge from a complex but orderly process. (A chart of the organizational structure appears as Appendix C.) This is particularly true of its social and political pronouncements and of its programs to promote justice and freedom. The WCC speaks with words and deeds. Its words have varying degrees of authority, depending on the issuing agency. When it speaks with deeds—and this usually means with money—the full authority of the organization stands behind it.

The highest authoritative body of the WCC is the Assembly, which meets every six or seven years. There have been five:

1. Amsterdam, Holland, 1948
2. Evanston, Illinois, 1954
3. New Delhi, India, 1961
4. Uppsala, Sweden, 1968
5. Nairobi, Kenya, 1975

These Assemblies make the major decisions about the character and direction of the WCC's work, in matters both of Faith and Order and of Church and Society. The Assemblies include delegates from all member churches, apportioned roughly according to size; the last Assembly, at Nairobi in 1975, had 676. Between Assemblies the authoritative agency is the Central Committee, which meets at twelve- or eighteen-month intervals. The Central Committee has approximately 135 members, elected by the Assembly. At present, representatives from Third World and Marxist states outnumber those from Western states in the Committee. Between Central Committee meetings, its Executive Committee, which consists of 25-30 members, may act in its behalf.

Four other elements of the World Council also play a policymaking role: (1) its six concurrent presidents, who are from different geographical regions and ecclesiastical traditions; (2) special standing bodies, such as the Commission of the Churches on International Affairs and the Program to Combat Racism; (3) WCC-supported meetings, such as the World Conference on Church and Society, held in Geneva in 1966; and (4) the Secretariat at the Geneva headquarters, which serves all elements of the WCC and as of December 1978 had a staff of approximately 275. The World Council also maintains a largely informational office in New York City with a staff of seven.

In a formal sense the World Council of Churches operates by Western democratic procedures. Each delegate to an Assembly and each member of the Central Committee has one vote, and issues are decided by majority rule. It is important to note, however, that the WCC headquarters staff is highly influential because it determines the agendas for discussion, develops project proposals, plans conferences and proposes themes, commissions preparatory materials and selects authors, and in general employs the means available to the senior staff in a large organization.

The World Council speaks with different levels of authority and degrees of consensus. An Assembly or the Central Committee may simply *receive* a report from a study group or special commission and commend it to the churches for their consideration, or it may *adopt* the report as a policy statement. In addressing current issues, the Executive Committee of the Central Committee may act in its own name, or the six WCC presidents may act in theirs. In certain situations, the WCC's general secretary, who is its chief executive officer, may speak in his own name.

Outsiders usually do not distinguish the actual level of authority behind a particular WCC pronouncement. This is not serious, however, because a significant degree of consensus exists among the statements issued by the various WCC units, a consensus rooted in the similarity of outlook among the senior staff in Geneva. The present study focuses on the authoritative pronouncements of the Assemblies but occasionally refers to statements by the Central Committee. The *actions* of the WCC—e.g., appropriations related to Third World interests—are taken at the highest levels of organizational authority.

The Two Meanings of "Third World"

The term "Third World" came into usage in the early 1950s to distinguish the countries of Asia, Africa, and Latin America from the Western world and the Communist world. The concept has come to have two meanings, the first largely geographical and the second ideological. In the first sense, the Third World embraces a great diversity of states in various stages of political and economic development short of the modern industrial society. Some of these states claim to pursue a policy of nonalignment in the East-

West struggle; but many of them in fact are tilted toward either the West or the Communist bloc, several wobble back and forth, and a score in Latin America have security ties with the United States under the Rio Pact of 1947. And some states claiming Third World status are Communist, such as Cuba and Vietnam. Hence, even in this geographical sense, the term "Third World" is pragmatic and ambiguous, covering a variety of non-Communist and near-Communist states, including several with relatively advanced economies, like Brazil, but excluding Japan, Australia, and New Zealand.[7]

Most Third World states have pluralistic societies made up of several, and sometimes many, racial, ethnic, and religious groups, frequently in rivalry or conflict with one another. Their governments tend to be weak and fragile and are often dominated by a privileged class or ethnic group. Most such regimes are authoritarian, and their leaders, seeking to maintain themselves in power and to modernize simultaneously, guarantee few of the political and civil rights taken for granted in the democratic West.

In the past fifteen years, "Third World" has taken on a second and more ideological meaning. It focuses on grievances against the West, real or alleged, and insists that many or most of the peoples in the geographical Third World have been oppressed by Western colonial powers in the past and are now being oppressed by "neo-colonialism," by transnational corporations, or even by formerly "imperialist" Christian missionary efforts. In this sense the term "Third World" is almost synonymous with the plight of people who are hungry, neglected, or oppressed. Thus the blacks, the Indians, and the Hispanics in the United States are members of the Third World because they, too, are seen as victims of oppression.

The geographical and the ideological definition of the Third World have both played a part in the unfolding story of the World Council of Churches, though gradually the ideological concept has come to the fore. The WCC seems to have been increasingly influenced by a Third World stereotype, a romanticized vision of how downtrodden people struggling for freedom, dignity, and economic development can gain a greater share of the world's power. Once "liberation" is achieved, in this view, a period of stern political control is justified until the situation matures to the point where a fuller range of human rights can be permitted.

The WCC was born a creature of the West. The great majority of its founders were from Protestant churches in Western Europe and North America. Gradually, as Asia and Africa were decolonized and the "newer" churches from these regions, as well as from Latin America, entered the WCC, the complexion of the organization and its outlook changed. It paid more attention to the Third World and became more responsive to demands made by church and secular spokesmen from the "developing" states and by Western representatives who spoke up for Third World causes. This development is not unlike that which took place in the General Assembly of the United Nations as it increased its membership from the original 60 in 1950 to 149 in 1978. Within the World Council, each delegate has one vote; in the U.N. General Assembly, each delegation has one vote. Hence both institutions became to some extent instruments for the voice and will of their Third World constituencies.

Questions to Be Addressed

The operation and program of the WCC, especially as they relate to Third World concerns, raise several crucial questions: *For* whom does the WCC speak? Does it speak and act for the member churches? Or does it speak and act only for itself? And *to* whom does the Council speak? Does it speak only to the churches and individual Christians, or also to governments and to the world?

Only in a vague and symbolic sense does the WCC speak for *all* its member churches. And it certainly could never speak for the millions of members of its member churches. Its pronouncements are addressed to the churches and to individual Christians, as well as to the world—more specifically, to particular governments or secular agencies whose behavior it seeks to encourage or modify.

The relation between the man or woman in the pew and the WCC Assembly differs significantly from the relation between an American voter and the U.S. Congress. The latter body is far more responsive to its constituency than any organ of the WCC is to its. Church members do not in any direct democratic sense choose their denomination's delegates to a WCC Assembly or its members—if any—on the Central Committee. These decisions of the constituent churches, like the decisions of the WCC itself, are made largely by the Executive Committee or the Central Committee, which in turn reflect senior staff influence. In the area of Church and Society, which deals with public issues, the decisions are in the main determined by what might be called the "social action establishment," the denominational and WCC staff members concerned with social and political questions. The establishment's views are usually ratified by the WCC voting bodies.

This raises a further question: Does the WCC, or any particular denomination for that matter, have the right to take a position that runs counter to the majority views of its members? It is generally acknowledged that many WCC pronouncements contradict the majority opinion within the member churches. Does this mean that these pronouncements lack authority?

The usual reply is that the WCC should make a "prophetic witness" rather than represent a current consensus, and that pronouncements should not hesitate to condemn the status quo and to call for reform or radical change, even if most church members continue to oppose the idea. The moral authority or political wisdom of a statement, according to this view, derives from the merit of the statement itself rather than from any democratic consensus. Consequently, church members, the public generally, and governments or other agencies to whom pronouncements are addressed should recognize that any wisdom or foolishness in a particular statement should *not* be attributed to the millions of Christians in whose name the WCC symbolically presumes to speak, but whom it cannot in any democratic sense claim to represent. Further, as Archbishop Temple said as early as 1938, no ecumenical statement has binding force on any member church.

The WCC has been criticized not only for taking stands that run counter to the majority views of its members but also for making pronouncements on specific issues without adequately examining the underlying theological and ethical principles. And it has been faulted by Paul Ramsey and others for frequently ignoring the most reliable empirical information available and turning, instead, to the diagnosis and prescriptions of secular ideologies, including those influenced by Marxism.[8]

We will address these charges in chapter 5 after a survey of the actual record of the WCC's concern for and action on behalf of Third World interests and demands. This is a selective account, focusing on the Third World theme with only occasional attention to collateral topics. The three middle chapters, largely chronological and descriptive, cover these periods: (2) The Responsible Society: 1948-1965; (3) Toward a More Radical Stance: 1966-1968; and (4) Triumph of Liberation Theology: 1969-1979. Special attention will be given to the Program to Combat Racism in chapters 4 and 5, because more than any other WCC endeavor it highlights the problems of relating the Christian ethic to conflicting political forces. The final chapter will evaluate the behavior of the WCC, both in word and in deed, by the Christian traditions it presumes to represent and by the moral quality and political consequences of its activity in support of justice, freedom, and human dignity in the Third World.

CHAPTER TWO

The Responsible Society: 1948-1965

Some nations are rejoicing in new freedom and power, some are bitter because freedom is denied them, some are paralyzed by division, and everywhere there is an undertone of fear.

MESSAGE OF THE AMSTERDAM ASSEMBLY, 1948[1]

THE INAUGURAL ASSEMBLY of the World Council of Churches in August 1948 convened in Amsterdam in a festive mood of postwar reconstruction, renewal, and high expectation. The Dutch capital had been spruced up to celebrate the jubilee of Queen Wilhelmina and the investiture of Princess Juliana. For the first time since the Nazis were driven from the Netherlands, Dutch citizens and foreigners alike were able to view the magnificently restored collection of Rembrandt paintings in the Royal Museum.

The Amsterdam Assembly was the most representative gathering of Christian churches in history. It drew 350 delegates from 150 churches in 43 countries, representing nearly all the Protestant denominations in the world as well as the Anglican, Greek Orthodox, and Old Catholic. The Roman Catholic and Russian Orthodox churches were not represented. After ten years as a provisional body, the World Council of Churches was voted into being at the first plenary session.

"Man's Disorder and God's Design" was the theme of the Assembly, but at Amsterdam, political disorder was more evident than God's design. The hostility toward Germany of Christians in formerly occupied lands had abated though not disappeared; a rally of 10,000 Dutch young people gave a standing ovation to Pastor Martin Niemöller (who had spent years in the Dachau concentration camp) after he delivered a stirring speech, the first public address in the German tongue given in the Netherlands since the war's end. But as old wounds were healing, new and deeper conflicts were beginning to emerge. The familiar labels of victor and defeated, liberated and neutral, were giving way to the new language of the East-West conflict—Western democracy vs. Communism, Marxism vs. capitalism. The emerging Cold War was symbolized by two assembly speakers, John Foster Dulles, a Presbyterian layman who later became U.S. secretary of state, and Professor Josef L. Hromádka, a churchman who was then a member of the Central Action Committee of Communist Czechoslovakia; each of them spoke on "Christian Responsibility in Our Divided World."

Western Orientation

At Amsterdam and for a decade and a half thereafter, the dominant themes, concerns, and leaders of the WCC were Western, primarily European and North American. Its chief concerns in 1948 included reestablishing ties between church leaders in the Allied and Axis states, helping with reconstruction in Europe, aiding refugees and prisoners of war, and defining the character of responsible nationalism. From the beginning, there was a small and growing interest in the "younger churches" of Asia and Latin America, and later of Africa. But delegates from these churches filled only two-thirds of the fifty seats reserved for them at Amsterdam. Africa, Asia, and Latin America were still "mission fields," and many of their Christian groups were organic parts of the denominations of Europe and North America rather than autonomous churches.

The Assembly addressed the ideological, political, and moral conflict between the Communist East and the democratic West but took a modest view of the church's ability to shape political or economic systems:

> The Church cannot resolve the debate between those who feel that the primary solution is to socialize the means of production and those who fear that such a course will merely lead to new and inordinate combinations of political and economic power, culminating finally in an omnicompetent State. In light of the Christian understanding of man we must, however, say to the advocates of socialization that the institution of property is not the root of the corruption of human nature. We must equally say to the defenders of existing property relations that ownership is not an unconditional right; it must, therefore, be preserved, curtailed or distributed in accordance with the requirements of justice.[2]

After reviewing points of conflict between capitalism and Communism, the Assembly pronounced a plague on both houses:

> The Christian churches should reject the ideologies of both Communism and *laissez-faire* capitalism, and should seek to draw men away from the false assumption that these extremes are the only alternatives. Each has made promises which it could not redeem. Communist ideology puts the emphasis upon economic justice, and promises that freedom will come automatically after the completion of the revolution. Capitalism puts the emphasis upon freedom, and promises that justice will follow as a by-product of free enterprise; that, too, is an ideology which has been proved false. It is the responsibility of Christians to seek new, creative solutions which never allow either justice or freedom to destroy the other.[3]

Toward a "Responsible Society"

The Assembly refrained from defining an acceptable halfway house between socialism and capitalism and declined to recommend any specific political or economic structures, though it clearly came down on the side of peaceful and constitutional change. Its basic political message was embraced in its definition of a "responsible society":

> A responsible society is one where freedom is the freedom of men who acknowledge responsibility to justice and public order, and where those who hold political authority or economic power are responsible for its exercise to God and the people whose welfare is affected by it.
>
> Man must never be made a mere means for political or economic ends. . . . It is required that the people have freedom to control, to criticize and to change their governments, that power be made responsible by law and tradition, and be distributed as widely as possible through the whole community. It is required that economic justice and provision of equality of opportunity be established for all the members of society.[4]

The definition was clarified by the Second Assembly, held in Evanston, Illinois, in 1954:

> Responsible society is not an alternative social or political system, but a criterion by which we judge all existing social orders and at the same time a standard to guide us in the specific choices we have to make. Christians are called to live responsibly, to live in response to God's act of redemption in Christ, in any society, even within the most unfavorable social structures.[5]

At the WCC-sponsored World Conference on Church and Society (Geneva, 1966), W. A. Visser 't Hooft—a Dutch theologian who was the first WCC general secretary—proposed the concept "responsible men participating in a world society in which all accept responsibility for the common welfare."[6] And two years later, at the Fourth Assembly (Uppsala, 1968), the phrase "responsible *world* society" was introduced. Visser 't Hooft gave substance to it by observing that the Amsterdam Assembly had emphasized economic justice *within* nations while by the mid-1960s the crucial issue was perceived as *international* economic justice.[7]

Perhaps the most articulate voice urging WCC attention to the emerging and volatile Third World at Amsterdam was that of M. M. Thomas, a leader of India's Mar Thoma Church. In his pre-Amsterdam report on Asia, Thomas said: "The attempt of the West to see western society and its disorders in isolation from Asia has necessarily falsified every interpretation of the crisis in the West."[8] He criticized the negative impact of the West on the society and economy of Asia and acknowledged the attractiveness of Marxism to many Asians. He also anticipated Christian participation in armed struggles against Western colonial power in Indonesia, Indochina, and elsewhere.

Little of Thomas's paper found its way into "The Church and the Disorder of Society," though that report did note that "the proclamation of racial equality by communists and their support of the cause of colonial peoples makes a strong appeal to the populations of Asia and Africa and to racial minorities everywhere." It also stated:

Christians should recognize with contrition that many churches are involved in the forms of economic injustice and racial discrimination which have created the conditions favorable to the growth of Communism, and that the atheism and the anti-religious teachings of Communism are in part a reaction to the checkered record of a professedly Christian society.[9]

Colonialism, Human Rights, and Korea

Amsterdam's condemnation of colonialism and racism was mild:

We . . protest against the exploitation of non-self-governing peoples for selfish purposes; the retarding of their progress toward self-government; and discrimination or segregation on the grounds of race or color.[10]

The WCC assumed that the Western colonial powers would grant self-determination and would promote constructive political and economic development by encouraging constitutional democracies, providing technical assistance, and transferring resources:

> Justice demands that the inhabitants of Asia and Africa, for instance, should have the benefits of more machine production. They may learn to avoid the mechanization of life and other dangers of an unbalanced economy which impair the social health of the older industrial peoples.[11]

The Assembly's Declaration on Religious Liberty, while addressed primarily to the West, was universally applicable and laid the foundation for the growing secular and religious concern for human rights.

East Asia was the first non-Western region into which the WCC took its quest for "the responsible society." The choice was pragmatic: the Council knew more Christian leaders there than in Africa or in largely Roman Catholic Latin America. This new interest was symbolized by the creation in 1951 of a joint WCC–International Missionary Council body, an East Asia Secretariat in Bangkok, Thailand. In the following year the WCC's Central Committee met in Lucknow, India, and its Study Department organized a Church and Society Conference there. The conference voiced distress over U.S. policy toward Asia, which it regarded as excessively anti-Communist in the wake of Mao's victory in China.

Two years earlier, however, the Central Committee had approved the United Nations' military response (led by the United States) to meet North Korean "aggression" (the Committee's word) across the thirty-eighth parallel. Its July 1950 statement on Korea precipitated a major internal controversy. T. C. Chao, a prominent Chinese ecumenical leader since the 1920s, resigned as a WCC president, and member churches in East Europe accused the Central Committee of abrogating political neutrality. Paul Bock continues the story in *In Search of a Responsible World Society*, a sympathetic history of the Church and Society emphasis in the ecumenical movement:

> Visser 't Hooft [the WCC general secretary] answered the charges by pointing out that the freedom of the churches to judge all systems does not impose on them the obligation to remain neutral, but rather the obligation to condemn injustice wherever it is found. By supporting the United Nations, the WCC was supporting the only instrument capable of bringing about international order. [Josef] Hromádka [of Czechoslovakia] responded that the UN is also an instrument of power politics, and, in this case, of the West.[12]

The early Central Committees clearly opposed the expansion of Communism, Soviet or Chinese, and saw no reason to expect good from a totalitarian system.

Evanston Assembly (1954): Emergence of the Third World

The WCC 1954 Assembly in Evanston showed a growing concern for the "underdeveloped countries" and acknowledged the revolutionary upheaval in Asia, Africa, and Latin America. The principal focus, however, continued to be on the East-West conflict, particularly the question of strategic arms control in view of the Soviet Union's explosion of a hydrogen bomb in 1950. The Assembly advocated international controls to bring about "the elimination and prohibition of atomic, hydrogen and all other weapons of mass destruction, as well as the reduction of all armaments to a minimum."[13] This statement bears out my comment at the time: "Sweeping goals and specific demands were set forth with little regard for the possibility of their achievement."[14] At the very least, the pronouncements reflected a confusion between aspiration and political achievement, and did not come to grips with what Reinhold Niebuhr has called "the relevance of the impossible ideal."

Evanston went far beyond Amsterdam in condemning colonialism and racism, two issues of considerable interest to the Third World. By 1954, India, Pakistan, Burma, Ceylon, and Indonesia had been granted independence. The Mau Mau rebellion raged in Kenya. Ho Chi Minh was fighting the French in Indochina. At the same time, peaceful plans for independence were under way in Nigeria, Ghana, Sierra Leone, Somalia, and other parts of Africa. Evanston called on the colonial powers to "remove the yoke which now prevents other nations and people from freely determining their own government and form of society."[15] The report on international affairs noted that "the older types of colonialism and imperialism are surely dying out" but that "new forms of imperialism call for vigilance," an oblique reference to Communist expansion. It expressed admiration for efforts by the "more developed countries" to give technical assistance to newly independent states.[16] Another report, however, said that the capital flow from colonial powers to newly independent states had dried up, making weak states weaker because "private investors hesitate to enter the scene without specific guarantees, and public funds without political strings attached are hard to procure."[17]

Evanston anticipated a rise in the standard of living in the Third World as rich countries made "increasing sacrifice."[18] Churches were urged to recruit Christian technicians and administrators to serve in U.N. agencies "meeting the needs of . . . underdeveloped countries."[19] While the Assembly warned against the abuse of government power, it also stressed the desirability of state planning:

> When necessary in the public interest, the state must intervene to prevent any center of economic or social power which represents partial interest from becoming stronger than itself, for the state alone has the power and the authority under God to act as trustee for society as a whole.[20]

By the early 1970s, the WCC considered the state's prerogative in social planning a central feature of "the responsible society" in the Third World. Thus it could sanction certain "nationalist" movements seeking power it would earlier have found abhorrent, such as those in Mozambique and Angola, which were not only authoritarian but anti-religious as well.

The Evanston report and resolutions on racial and ethnic tensions fueled a continuing campaign to wipe out racial discrimination. The report said: "Racial and ethnic fears, hates and prejudices are more than social problems. . . . They are sins against God and His commandments."[21] Some impetus for the anti-racism stand came from Asia and Africa, but a more immediate incentive was the growing civil-rights movement in the United States.

Evanston authorized a special secretariat to implement the report on racial tensions, but the mandate lay dormant for six years. Finally, in 1960, after several studies on how to help churches troubled with racism, the Central Committee invited Daisuke Kitagawa, an American Episcopal priest, to head a Secretariat on Racial and Ethnic Relations. It was not given a budget until the 1961 New Delhi Assembly, which also adopted a set of operating principles. Lacking authority, the secretariat merged into the Program to Combat Racism after the 1968 Uppsala Assembly.

New Delhi Assembly (1961): "Rapid Social Change"

The phrase "rapid social change" was used repeatedly in the preparatory paper on underdeveloped countries for Evanston and was elaborated at the New Delhi Assembly in 1961. It continues to be used in WCC circles as a rough synonym for conditions of social disorder (or revolution) caused by either "development" or "underdevelopment," depending on one's perspective.

In 1954, the WCC's Department of Church and Society began a study on "The Common Christian Responsibility Toward Areas of Rapid Social Change." Initial funding of $100,000 from John D. Rockefeller Jr. and $25,000 from the Phelps-Stokes Fund was augmented by contributions from member churches. Clearly focused on the Third World, the study called for action in several areas, including (1) political independence and nationalism, (2) industrial and urban development, and (3) rural and village life. The churches and countries of the West were assigned major tasks in the response to rapid change in Africa, Asia, and Latin America, "since they have helped to bring it about."[22]

Although the project did not elicit great enthusiasm from the West during its first five years, there was enough support to move ahead. By the time of the New Delhi Assembly (1961), "rapid social change" had become the subject of many consultations in the Third World, and it was to be a major concern at the World Conference on Church and Society in 1966.

The New Delhi Assembly was the first one held outside the Northern Hemisphere. Here the WCC accepted eighteen new member churches from the Third World, eleven of them from Africa. Conditions seemed ripe for the Amsterdam slogan "the responsible society" to be invested with a more revolutionary meaning. Paul Abrecht, a prime mover behind the "Rapid Social Change" study, noted, however, that the churches in 1961 could do this and cope with a variety of public issues only in a conference devoted entirely to Church and Society concerns.[23]

The admission of the Third World churches at New Delhi was over-shadowed by the entry of the Russian Orthodox Church and its sister bodies in Bulgaria, Rumania, and Poland. At a time when arms-limitation talks were complicated by the Berlin and Cuban crises, some WCC leaders hoped the Orthodox involvement would somehow help to improve East-West relations.

The major Third World issue at New Delhi was Portugal's role in Angola. During 1961 there were several insurrections by nationalist groups against Portuguese policies or rule. After the first revolt, in northern Angola, its leader, Holden Roberto, deplored the "extreme violence" of his followers, which had led to the killing of perhaps 750 Portuguese settlers.[24] These excesses set the stage for severe military action by Portuguese authorities in which thousands of Africans were reportedly killed. The WCC Executive Committee criticized Portuguese policy and endorsed political self-determination for Angola's black majority.

A similar resolution polarized the New Delhi Assembly. Its supporters said the WCC should condemn Portugal for its repressive colonial policy; opponents argued that the WCC should not single out a particular state for censure. The vote was 179 for and 177 against the resolution. In a compromise, the Assembly "associated itself" with the Executive Committee's statement without saying anything on its own. The basic disagreement was not over Angola—few if any delegates supported Portugal's policies in Africa—but over the matter of condemning a specific government. The delegates were split on the issue, and the time-honored practice of confining Assembly pronouncements to the enunciation of principles was being eroded. To this day, the issue of specific condemnations has not been fully resolved.

Two embryonic ideas emerged at New Delhi that would later influence the WCC's stance toward the Third World. The first was an implicit acceptance of "temporary authoritarian regimes" as guarantors of social order and economic development. To be sure, supporters of such regimes were to be informed that "power corrupts," and Christians were admonished not to acquiesce to "old or new forms of tyranny."[25] Full human rights remained the goal, but New Delhi acknowledged that they may have to be restricted to fit the degree of political, social, and economic maturity in developing countries. "It is possible for a Christian to live (or die) with integrity under any political system; it is possible for the Church to obey its Lord in all kinds of external circumstances."[26]

Second, the report of the Commission of the Churches on International Affairs contained the faint outlines of what later came to be called the New International Economic Order. It dealt briefly with international economic cooperation, U.N. development aid, fair trade policies, price stabilization of major commodities and manufactured goods, training and research in development, and population control.[27]

CHAPTER THREE

Toward a More Radical Stance: 1966-1968

In their death agonies . . . the western Churches are distributing the causes of their own sickness—the politicization of religion— to their healthy offspring in the developing world.

EDWARD NORMAN[1]

DURING THE SEVEN YEARS between the New Delhi Assembly in 1961 and the Uppsala Assembly in 1968, the World Council of Churches virtually moved from a "theology of order" and peaceful change to a "theology of revolution."[2] From Amsterdam (1948) through New Delhi, the WCC asserted that the disordered world was to be transformed into "the responsible society" by accepting God's design. At Uppsala the disorder and the design were melded together. As the familiar foundations were shaken by the hand of God, Christians celebrated the tremors from which a new humanity would be born.

This radical and rapid change in the Council's worldview was the product of both external and internal forces. In part, the WCC was caught up in the revolutionary ferment in Western intellectual circles, and in this it both reflected and stimulated a similar outlook among its representatives from the Third World. This shift of focus was thus not simply the result of increasing representation in the WCC from Asia, Africa, and Latin America. The Third World outlook and constituency, as noted in chapter 1, had been developed largely in the United States and Europe; then it was exported to the Third World. To be sure, there was communication between Third World nationalists and Western reformers, but the latter provided the motivating ideas and example. Black militants in Watts and

21

Washington made common cause with European student activists in speaking out on Third World grievances. They all were persuaded that economic and political "repression" south of the equator could not end short of revolution at home and abroad. For them the Third World was not simply a geographical area or an economic problem but fundamentally a symbol of universal "repression."

Richard John Neuhaus has accused the WCC of practicing "a kind of colonialism, or neocolonialism, of the Left in selecting the voices it wishes to hear from the Third World":

> I recall a recent WCC consultation in Switzerland on Christian faith and ideology at which the dominant voices were professed advocates of Marxist or quasi-Marxist revolutionism. A black participant from Nigeria took exception to this line and was promptly informed by a "liberation theologian" representing a minuscule part of Protestantism in Latin America that he, the Nigerian churchman, did not represent "*the* Third World viewpoint." Nobody on the WCC staff expressed any misgivings about this imposition of a "viewpoint" upon two-thirds of the world [italics added].[3]

The increasingly radical trend in the World Council's social and political positions was made dramatically manifest in the WCC-sponsored Conference on Church and Society, held in Geneva, Switzerland, in July 1966. It came to full bloom in the fourth WCC Assembly, which took place in Uppsala, Sweden, in mid-1968.

Geneva Conference (1966): Reform to Revolution?

Disappointed with the New Delhi Assembly's inability to come to grips with the theological and political implications of "dynamic change" in the Third World, WCC Church and Society officials decided to stage a less inhibited, semi-autonomous conference in the old Life and Work tradition. Thus the World Conference on Church and Society was convened in Geneva in mid-1966 under the theme "Christians in the Technical and Social Revolutions of Our Time."

The Geneva Conference drew some 360 delegates from 80 countries and 164 churches. In two weeks they adopted more than a hundred paragraphs of "conclusions" on a bewildering variety of complex issues. The prevailing mood was pro–Third World and anti-American. Historian-columnist John P. Roche, then a special consultant to President Johnson, observed that at times the Geneva Conference led one to suspect that "anti-Americanism" had "become a substitute for the Nicene Creed as the focus of Christian unity."[4]

At Geneva the mood of guilt among the delegates from the rich and powerful West encouraged representatives from the Third World to voice their outrage. Most U.S. delegates accepted the charges of oppression and neo-imperialism against America, and some even insisted that the charges were not strong enough. Peter Kirk, a British M.P. and an old ecumenical hand, observed that this was not the first time he had seen the "remarkable American propensity for self-flagellation."[5] In fact, zealous Western reformers viewed with suspicion any Third World delegates who failed to blame the West for all their miseries past and present.

The Geneva Conference did not enjoy the authority of a WCC Assembly because it could speak only *to* the churches and the WCC and not *for* them. The planners sought geographical and professional diversity, but at the same time their selection of speakers and delegates—the latter from names submitted by the churches—virtually ensured a call for radical political change. There was rough equality between Western and Third World delegations. The voting participants included 76 Western Europeans, 65 North Americans, 46 Asians, 45 from the Soviet Union and Eastern Europe, 42 Latin Americans, 42 Africans, 17 from the Middle East, and 5 from Australia and New Zealand. Of these 338 delegates, 158 were theologians and clergymen and 180 were laymen, many of whom had political experience or were expert in the natural or social sciences. The official conference report lists "50 political leaders and civil servants, 19 businessmen and industrialists, 28 economists, 36 professional men, 9 workers or trade union leaders, 20 social scientists and 8 natural scientists."[6] Given the conference conclusions, it appears that in most professional categories delegates were chosen, in part, because of their ideological preference for "rapid social change."

In accordance with the mood of the conference, the black civil-rights leader Martin Luther King, Jr., was asked to preach at the Sunday worship service. This he did by means of a film flown in from Chicago. Some forty other persons also spoke, about half from the United States and Western Europe. The majority of the others were from the Third World. There was some diversity among them. Paul Bock observed:

> The delegates from Asia and Africa showed little interest in the theory of Communism. They were looking for a practical and convincing revolutionary concept of social development. . . . Insofar as Marxist categories were helpful in diagnosing the problems of capitalism and in providing an idea of the good society, many were willing to use them.[7]

One of the most discussed speeches was by Bola Ige of Nigeria, an attorney who formerly led the Christian Student Movement in his country. The initial euphoria of new states carved out of the European colonial empires, Ige said, had given way to serious doubts about just how much freedom they had achieved. The new states were learning that "political freedom and economic emancipation are intertwined—no nation can really have one without the other."[8] New states, he added, are demanding "a share of the power now concentrated in the minority." He lashed out at all who advocated gradual reform and who supported revolutionary change only within constitutional limits, calling for world revolution to "knock out all existing suffocating constitutions, systems and the powers that keep them going."[9]

Eduardo Mondlane, a founder of the "liberation" struggle against Portugal in Africa, was perhaps even more radical: he advised Third World countries to look after themselves. Mondlane had no demands to lay on the superpowers except that Third World peoples should be left alone to sort out their identities. He was passionately confident that they could shape their own societies—even if that meant remaining poor for a long time.

Mondlane was later hailed by the WCC as a major speaker at Geneva, but his radical position on self-determination coupled with self-sufficiency made little impact on the conference. Ige's tirade was more attractive. It whetted the guilt feelings of the Westerners and prompted them to call on individual Christians and the churches to liberate the oppressed.

There were many variations on four principal themes at Geneva:

1. *The gap between rich and poor states should be closed.* This would require a New International Economic Order in which the developed nations would contribute 1 to 2 per cent of their annual GNP to aid the underdeveloped, tariff barriers against the Third World would be removed, safeguards against domination by foreign capital would be established, and the prices of commodities would be stabilized. These measures would lead to land reform and industrialization in developing countries.

2. *States must control all centers of power within them.* Geneva was more leary than the Evanston Assembly of viewing the state as the sole legal authority under God. Between 1954 and 1966, the issues of civil disobedience and conscientious objection had raised basic questions about the power of the state in the West. Yet Geneva had no trouble assigning full power to governments to determine economic policy and to control all other centers of power "for the common good."[10]

3. The new nationalism of Third World states is different from the old nationalism that led to war. The former is a vehicle of social integration, while "aggressive nationalisms" of the West "deify the nation and provoke feelings of national superiority."[11]

4. Revolutionary violence is permissible as a last resort in overthrowing oppressive elites if it will eliminate "the vast covert violence which the existing order involves."[12] This judgment emerged from a long debate that began with the Amsterdam Assembly's assertion that "war is contrary to the will of God." The debate still continues.

Whatever else may be said of the Geneva Conference, it clearly signaled a crucial turning point in the World Council's view of the West and its responsibilities to the Third World. It was regarded as a milestone by its planners.

The mood and positions of the Geneva Conference also drew many criticisms. The French Reformed sociologist Jacques Ellul, who spoke at Geneva, was later highly critical: "The World Council precipitately adopted positions that seemed to me scarcely worth taking seriously: problems poorly analyzed, inadequate solutions, superficiality, lack of sound theological thinking. . . . I have a horror of the reign of false experts!"[13] After Geneva, Ellul ceased to participate in the WCC, which he had helped to found.

Another critic was Paul Ramsey, a professor of religion and ethics at Princeton University, who was an observer-consultant at Geneva. His book *Who Speaks for the Church?*, published in 1967, is a trenchant and far-reaching analysis of the Geneva Conference and of the World Council's efforts to influence the political order.[14] Ramsey denounced the Protestant "passion for numerous particular pronouncements"; it reflects, he said, a confusion over the proper spheres of church and state. He attacked the substance of many of the Geneva statements, the process that produced them, and the assumptions that underlay them. Carl F. H. Henry, the founding editor of the evangelical fortnightly *Christianity Today*, called Ramsey's book "an ecumenical bombshell" and commended him for laying bare "the worst incursion of churchmen into political affairs since the Middle Ages."

Ramsey maintained that the churches have the right to speak out on great moral issues such as tyranny, genocide, and wars of conquest, but he said it was morally wrong and politically foolish for them to give specific policy advice, such as urging that Communist China be admitted to the United Nations or condemning as unjust U.S. bombing in North and South

Vietnam. He added that the Geneva statement on Vietnam was one-sided, scandalously imprecise, and irresponsible, and that it increased public confusion about U.S. aims and the self-restraint it exercised in a complex situation.

As a regional follow-up to Geneva, the National Council of Churches in October 1967 sponsored a U.S. Conference on Church and Society, held in Detroit. The mood and stance of the two meetings were similar; if anything, Detroit's condemnation of U.S. policies in Vietnam and elsewhere was even stronger than Geneva's. The speeches and resolutions revealed a profound confusion between lawful coercion and lawless violence that encourages civil disobedience.

The Vietnam War

The mood of Western guilt noted above was further deepened by growing criticism of the American military effort to protect the territorial integrity of South Vietnam against the Moscow- and Peking-supported aggression of North Vietnam, and by all the political and moral ambiguities attending U.S. involvement in a protracted guerrilla war. From 1964 on, the U.S. role in Indochina did more than anything else to radicalize American students, familiarize them with Third World revolutionary forces, and turn them against the Western "military-industrial complex." The Vietnam issue also propelled the Third World into the consciousness of the Western church leaders who set the WCC agenda. It made a strong impact at the Geneva Conference, and it permeated the Uppsala Assembly two years later.

Geneva issued one of the first direct religious condemnations of the U.S. policy in Vietnam. Its views on Vietnam must be seen in the light of other statements on war, atomic weapons, and the obligation of major powers not to obstruct "the necessary changes" in the Third World, "not to give undue primacy to their own interests in stability, and not to interpret events in terms of their own ideological preoccupations."[15] A majority of the Geneva delegates agreed that U.S. military action in Vietnam was preventing necessary change in a new state and was motivated by an unjustified concern for ideology and stability. Geneva also said that the churches should challenge the policies of all belligerents, and it supported earlier WCC calls for the United States to stop bombing the North and for Hanoi to stop infiltrating the South. It urged an end to all hostilities so peace negotiations could begin.

Uppsala Assembly (1968): "All Things New"

Meeting under the banner "Behold, I Make All Things New," the WCC Assembly in Uppsala in mid-1968 attracted 904 delegates from 235 member churches. The agenda was virtually controlled by what Paul Ramsey has called "the social action curia," the Church and Society stalwarts from the staffs of the WCC and the major member denominations. Of the six study sections, four were devoted to the problems of "rapid social change."

Uppsala ratified the general approach of the Geneva Conference, though it did not act on all of Geneva's specific resolutions. On four central topics—racism, peace, social justice, and Third World development—Uppsala, according to some participants, was a kind of orgy of Western confessions of guilt, especially within the U.S. delegation. American participants professed embarrassment about their country's slow progress in civil rights, its involvement in Vietnam, its wealth, and its economic domination in the Third World, and about the continuing presence of white regimes in Africa. The Assembly called for "radical change," "economic justice," and "liberation." The moral burden for achieving these objectives fell most heavily on the United States and Western Europe.

Some resolutions affirmed the morality of revolutionary violence against "inhumane structures"; the struggles against Hitler in Germany and Batista in Cuba were cited as past examples of justified violence. But one Assembly section sanctioned only non-violent strategies for achieving justice. The ambiguity on this persistent issue was not resolved.

Uppsala did not, as is sometimes implied, skim over political and civil rights as defined in the West in a rush to affirm the "economic and social rights" (such as food, housing, and jobs) that are emphasized by Marxist states. All the human rights enumerated in the Universal Declaration and other U.N. documents were affirmed. Further, Uppsala called for equal status for women and "their full participation in human affairs." It championed the right of conscientious objection to all wars and to particular wars. It called for an international convention on religious liberty for individuals and groups. It vigorously asserted the rights of ethnic, cultural, and religious minorities. The Assembly went even further: while affirming the freedoms of speech, press, and religion, it placed beside them the right of the poor and powerless to development and self-determination. When individual rights and social-development rights were in conflict in a new state, Uppsala tilted toward postponing the first until the second were assured. Plans for liberation and development might have to be made by an elite group "before full democratic structures can be achieved."[16]

Third World economic development was the really new problem tackled at Uppsala. The Western industrial states were called selfish, stubborn, and sometimes neo-isolationist. The first "development decade" was declared a "decade of disillusionment," partly because the United States and Western Europe were inclined to reduce their financial and technical aid to developing states and refused to alter trade and investment patterns in order to help them. To close the gap between rich and poor and to move toward a New International Economic Order, Uppsala followed the lead of Geneva and recommended that by 1971 the industrialized powers increase their Third World development aid to at least 1 per cent of their GNP. Church members were urged to impose on themselves a voluntary development tax based on the difference between what their government was giving and what it *should* give to development.

Harsh language was directed against Third World elites that monopolize and profiteer at the expense of their people. In such situations churches were urged to take up the cause of the poor and to support revolution if necessary.

A statement on family planning and birth control created some difficulties. The Orthodox delegates felt the WCC should not pronounce on the matter. In a compromise, Uppsala noted that the population explosion has long-range implications for economic development, food production, and jobs, and that some churches and parents advocate the use of birth-control devices while others have moral objections to this practice.

The civil war in Nigeria presented a perplexing problem. On the one hand, the Ibo people of the Eastern Province (Biafra) charged that massive persecution and slaughter by federal Nigerian forces was the chief reason for their secession in May 1967, and the Biafran cause was recognized as just by many Western and Third World Christians. Aid to Biafra was a major humanitarian enterprise in Europe and North America. Heroes were made running the federal blockade. And Sir Francis Ibiam, one of Biafra's top leaders, was a president of the World Council. On the other hand, federal Nigeria had several churches in the WCC, and Biafra's secession was tearing apart the fabric of Nigerian nationalism. Before Uppsala, the WCC had raised $3.8 million in money and materials for both sides; but the division at the Assembly made it impossible to continue the aid because it would have conferred legitimacy on the Biafran cause.

On the Vietnam issue, the great majority of the 704 delegates believed that the United States was suppressing desirable revolutionary change. Only 20 delegates voted against and 30 abstained on a resolution that read in part: "The appalling situation of the Vietnamese people today offers an example of the tragedy to which unilateral intervention of a great power can lead. Moreover, such intervention creates rather than solves political, social and economic problems."[17] There was no condemnation of Soviet or Chinese support of North Vietnam's aggression against the South, though the Assembly called on "all parties" to "stop military actions in South Vietnam."

CHAPTER FOUR

Triumph of Liberation Theology: 1969-1979

Modern Christian leaders are all tolerant when it comes to departures from traditional religious doctrine. But they are ferocious when it comes to departures from the canons of liberalism. . . .

EDWARD NORMAN[1]

DURING THE LATTER PART of the turbulent decades between the Amsterdam Assembly (1948) and the Uppsala Assembly (1968), the World Council of Churches became increasingly receptive to the growing and controversial "liberation theology" movement that was then under way among Roman Catholics in Latin America. Years before their doctrinal foundation was ratified at the Assembly in Nairobi, Kenya, in 1975, the WCC "liberation theologians" had become involved in Third World politics. Their concern became abundantly manifest in the Council's vigorous Program to Combat Racism, which from 1970 through 1978 gave over $3 million to Marxist and other "liberation" groups and supporting organizations in Asia, Australasia, Latin America, the Caribbean, Europe, and North America.

The "liberation" effort, which has involved only a small portion of the WCC's budget and staff time (in 1979 the Program to Combat Racism had four staff members in a WCC headquarters staff of 275), has from the start been controversial. In significant respects it runs counter to the main theological stream of the Faith and Order tradition, which emphasizes doctrinal and ecclesiastical concerns. It also violates the political and religious views of the majority of members of the churches within the WCC, especially those in Europe and North America, who do not believe in violent, revolutionary change when peaceful alternatives for achieving greater justice, order, and freedom are available.

Among the WCC conferences in the 1970s that focused on the demands of Third World spokesmen and the duties of the industrial states were the "Salvation Today" conference (Bangkok, 1973), where "liberation" for many delegates became almost synonymous with salvation, and the World Conference on Science and Technology for Human Development (Bucharest, 1974).

A parallel and less controversial effort was the WCC's Commission on the Churches' Participation in Development. Organized in 1970, it had spent approximately $12 million by 1978. The main source of financing is church contributions, and by far the largest donors in recent years have been the churches in the Netherlands and West Germany. The Fund gives development grants for projects such as (in 1977) a self-help program for Australian aboriginal children, a marketing association for small manufacturers in India, and a cattle project among North American Indians. In 1975 the WCC joined with the Netherlands Council of Churches in forming the Ecumenical Cooperative Society, which now has 104 shareholders from six continents. The Society has assets of more than $1 million and has made several loans to Third World development projects, including $100,000 to an agricultural credit cooperative in Ecuador.

Program to Combat Racism

The Program to Combat Racism is rooted in the strong anti-racism pronouncements of the Uppsala Assembly in 1968 and in a recognition of the ineffectiveness of the WCC Secretariat on Racial and Ethnic Relations (established in 1961). Its direct impetus was a WCC consultation held in London in May 1969 under the chairmanship of U.S. Senator George McGovern, who had been a Methodist delegate at Uppsala. Though subjected to disruptions and abusive statements by an American Black Power group and white extremists, the London meeting succeeded in issuing proposals to eradicate racism—educational efforts, political and social action, economic sanctions against "racist" regimes, and moral and material support for groups fighting racism.

In response, the WCC Central Committee in 1969 authorized a five-year (later extended) Program to Combat Racism (PCR) that was to include study, consultative services to member churches, and a fund to help "organizations of oppressed racial groups or organizations supporting victims of racial injustice whose purposes are not inconsonant with the general purposes of the World Council" (see Appendixes E and G). The WCC grants were to be used by recipients "in their struggle for economic, social and political justice." Committee members voted an initial $200,000 from the general WCC budget for the fund and asked member churches for an additional $300,000.

The task of allocating grants was assigned to the Executive Committee of the WCC's Central Committee, and the first ones were announced in the fall of 1970. Nineteen secular activist groups (ten in Africa, the others in Australia, Japan, Colombia, and Europe) received small grants out of the initial $200,000. Of these, the following got $10,000 or more:

Angola: National Union for the Total Independence of Angola, People's Movement for the Liberation of Angola, Revolutionary Government of Angola in Exile; *Guinea-Bissau:* African Independence Party of Guinea and Cape Verde Islands; *Mozambique:* Mozambique Institute of FRE-LIMO; *Rhodesia:* Zimbabwe African National Union (ZANU), Zimbabwe African People's Union (ZAPU); *South Africa:* Lutuli Memorial Foundation of African National Congress; *Zambia:* Africa 2000 Project; *Australia:* Federal Council for the Advancement of Aborigines and Torres Strait Islanders, National Tribal Council; *Colombia:* Committee for the Defense of the Indian. Most of these groups were Marxist-led or -influenced.

The announcement of these grants stirred up a hornet's nest. Criticism focused on several African "liberation" movements armed and supported by the Soviet Union that were waging guerrilla warfare against Portuguese rule in Angola, Mozambique, and Guinea-Bissau.

Despite the outcry, the WCC continued the PCR grants. Council spokesmen acknowledged that some of the recipients were engaged in a military struggle (involving guerrilla war and terrorist tactics), but they pointed out that these groups also provided educational, health, and social services for the people they were "liberating." The grants were solely for humanitarian purposes, insisted the WCC, and were not used to buy guns.

From 1970 through 1978, the PCR gave $3,063,545 to more than a hundred organizations in some two dozen countries. Almost 65 per cent of this money went to guerrilla groups seeking to overthrow white regimes (and in Rhodesia and South West Africa-Namibia in 1978, interracial interim regimes) in southern Africa and to other organizations supporting political change there.

Program to Combat Racism: Grants, 1970-1978
In Current U.S. Dollars

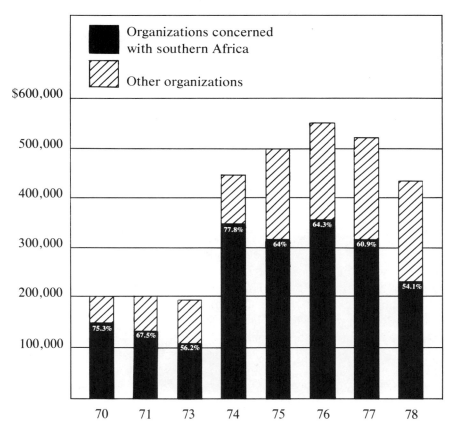

NOTE: The total granted during this nine-year period was $3,063,545, of which $1,979,545 (or 64.6%) was given to organizations in southern Africa or groups elsewhere supporting these organizations. No grants were appropriated in 1972. For details, see Appendix F.

After southern Africa, the next two most popular causes of the PCR, measured by the sizes of the grants, have been "liberating" blacks and "liberating" Indians in the United States and Canada. Only token assistance was given to scores of other "repressed" ethnic groups. The WCC's PCR grants break down geographically in this way (shown in thousands of U.S. dollars; no grants were given in 1972):

	1970	1971	1973	1974	1975	1976	1977	1978
Africa	135	130	101	322	257	275	265	180
Asia and Australasia	27	5	14	14	37.5	37.5	50	62
South America and the Caribbean	15	25	20	25	60	38	22.5	15
North America	. . .	30	41	49	73.5	106	95	90
Europe	23	10	18	40	72	103.5	92.5	87.5
TOTAL	200	200	194	450	500	560	525	434.5

As noted in chapter 1, the 1978 "humanitarian" grant of $85,000 to the so-called Patriotic Front engaged in guerrilla operations to overthrow the interim biracial regime in Rhodesia raised a storm of protest. Letters from angry church members and others flooded the WCC offices in Geneva. Sectors of the general and religious press were highly critical. The Salvation Army, the Presbyterian Church in Ireland, and a provincial Evangelical Lutheran Church in West Germany suspended their WCC membership in protest. The grant was criticized not only because the Front was supported by Cuba and the Soviet Union and one of its leaders was a declared Marxist, but because its forces deliberately murdered innocent civilians, including foreign missionaries, and because its entire campaign was aimed at destroying an interracial, peaceful, constitutional (though less than perfect) effort designed to establish an independent, democratic state in Rhodesia. As of July 31, 1978, just before the WCC announced its grants, the Front had murdered 207 white civilians and 1,712 black civilians, not counting 296 civilians killed by terrorist mines.

Dismissing all criticism of the grant to the Patriotic Front as invalid, the WCC a month later announced a grant of $125,000 to SWAPO, the Marxist-led guerrilla force then attempting to prevent the peaceful transition of South West Africa into an independent and democratic state, Namibia. The constitutional arrangements for this transition were overwhelmingly endorsed by a territory-wide election based on a universal adult franchise in December 1978. (Earlier that year the U.S. Senate expressed its disapproval of the "distribution of U.N. funds," 25 per cent from U.S. taxpayers, "to communist sponsored terrorist organizations such as SWAPO."[2]) This grant brought the total WCC aid to SWAPO to $498,500 (see Appendix F).

Acknowledging the "fierce attacks in the public media and in the church press, as well as from numerous local church groups, on the PCR grants," WCC General Secretary Philip Potter told the Central Committee, meeting in Kingston, Jamaica, in January 1979, that the WCC was "at a crossroads" in its relations with its member churches but that God's rule demanded "a radical change of economic, social, and political structures."[3] He noted that three churches had suspended their membership and that "we have had to face the ugly spectacle that many persons in our major contributing churches are clamoring for reduction or withdrawal of support . . . if they disagree strongly with particular actions of the Council." (See Appendix I.)

In the debate, speakers critical of the grants—including representatives from the Anglican Church of Ireland, the Salvation Army, and the Lutheran Church of Norway, and André Appel, general secretary of the Lutheran World Federation—were, according to one observer, "received in polite silence, whereas members expressing affirmation of the grants often received rounds of applause."[4] Given this prevailing mood, the outcome was predictable. The Committee on January 10 approved a report on the PCR that in effect ratified a four-page memorandum, "World Council Grants to Groups Combating Racism: Facts and Rationale," issued by the Council's New York office in August 1978. (This memorandum appears as Appendix G.)

The PCR report approved at Kingston concluded that the purpose and thrust of the program "are still valid" and that only "the adverse image" created by the controversial grants "needs to be changed."[5] In short, the contributions to Marxist-oriented guerrillas who were seeking to shoot their way into power were endorsed. The Central Committee "noted" the "criticisms voiced in good faith by some member churches." But it urged the churches to be wary:

Member churches should be helped to question the sources of information about PCR's activities and to examine press reports with critical judgement; for example, information issued by racist government agencies or censored by them, as well as by private organizations and published in religious and secular press. Attention should be given to terminology such as "execution," "assassination," "guerrilla," "terrorist," etc.

It concluded that the PCR grants so far had fulfilled the "criteria set by the Central Committee."

The Central Committee also reaffirmed its request that the PCR "give special attention to the issues of investments and trade . . . bank loans . . . to South Africa" because "foreign economic interests" were, it claimed, major supporters of apartheid. And it urged the PCR to intensify its efforts against "organized white mass migration from Southern Africa especially into those countries with racially oppressed peoples." Latin America was mentioned as vulnerable to the "transfer of racism" by white settlers from southern Africa. Combating "racism in Asia" was reaffirmed as a major concern for the PCR in 1979. The Central Committee also asked the PCR to "indicate a plan of action" on the issue of "land rights and racially oppressed indigenous peoples" in Australia and Brazil.

Several pertinent facts will help to place the controversial PCR grants in perspective. The program has never received widespread financial support from the member churches. During the first year, 1970, the WCC allocated $200,000 from its general funds without consulting its member churches on either the beneficiaries or the amounts of the grants. After that the grants were financed by gifts from interested individuals and groups. In 1974, the Executive Committee, in distributing $450,000 to twenty-nine organizations on six continents, announced that the money came only from "special contributions from churches and individuals supplemented by donations from the governments of Netherlands, Sweden, and Norway." (See Appendix G.) More than half of the American contributions to the PCR reportedly came from the United Methodist Church and the United Presbyterian Church.

In 1975 and 1976 the PCR gave $110,000 to two Rhodesian nationalist leaders, Bishop Abel Muzorewa and the Reverend Ndabaningi Sithole; but after the two joined Ian Smith in March 1978 in an interim interracial regime committed to the peaceful establishment of a democratic Rhodesia-Zimbabwe, they were blacklisted by the WCC as unworthy of further support. The official explanation was that the WCC never supported governments and that Muzorewa and Sithole were now a part of the regime. Since then the money has gone to their adversaries, Marxist terrorists who operate primarily from sanctuaries in Mozambique and Zambia. This suggests that the PCR grants are not given solely for humanitarian reasons. There are refugees and other human needs on both sides, so a genuine humanitarian effort would presumably be directed to both. On March 23, 1979, WCC General Secretary Potter issued a statement supporting the appeal of the International Committee of the Red Cross for full access to areas on both sides of the border to minister to the needs of the victims of the Rhodesian guerrilla war. (The United Methodist Church and other WCC member denominations, however, continued to give to mission and relief causes within Rhodesia, but not to Bishop Muzorewa.)

The WCC makes it abundantly clear that the PCR aid, in addition to serving humanitarian aims, is intended to make a political statement. Unlike the nonpolitical refugee assistance given by the WCC through Church World Service, which has earned widespread respect, these PCR grants took sides in the struggle over what forces would control the new regime in Rhodesia. One official WCC paper frankly states that the anti-racism grants are made to permit the Council to "move beyond charity and involve itself in the redistribution of power."[6] Recognizing this, the pro-ecumenical *Christian Century* was prompted to label Western Christians who "side with Zimbabweans who believe majority rule can be achieved only through armed struggle" as "armchair guerrillas and vicarious doers of violence."[7]

Violence, Justice, and Human Rights

Although the WCC spent considerable time in the 1970s discussing the relation between violence and the struggle for justice, its officers were reluctant to justify the substantial PCR grants to "liberation" groups in these terms. "Violence, Nonviolence and the Struggle for Justice," a study presented to the Central Committee in August 1973, addresses the ambiguities inherent in efforts to overcome evil and injustice. The report asserts that Christians may not condone or participate in the conquest of one people by another, in deliberate oppression by one class or race, or in the indiscriminate killing of innocent non-combatants in a war.[8] On the perplexing question of resisting "unjust and oppressive political or economic power" the report was not conclusive:

> Some believe that nonviolent action is the only possibility consistent with obedience to Jesus Christ. . . . Some are prepared to accept the necessity of violent resistance as a Christian duty in extreme circumstances. . . . Some find themselves already in situations of violence in which they cannot help but participate. Nonviolence does not present itself as an option unless they would withdraw totally from the struggle for justice.[9]

After a spirited debate in the Central Committee over the location of open or suppressed violence in the world, the WCC named the Republic of South Africa, the United States, Northern Ireland, the Middle East, and Latin America (no specific states were identified in the latter two areas). Some members questioned whether the list was balanced. "Is there no danger of violence in Eastern Europe?" asked a Norwegian bishop. An effort to add the Soviet satellites to the list was defeated. Other committee members asked about Western Europe, Asia, the Pacific, and black Africa.

The debate over identifying specific states troubled by violence illustrates a persistent problem for the WCC. Some observers charge that the Council continually jumps on the United States, South Africa, post-Allende Chile, South Korea, and the Philippines but says nothing about human-rights violations in the Soviet Union, China, Cambodia, Nigeria, Mozambique, Tanzania, and Cuba. Though there was frank criticism of the Soviet Union at the Nairobi Assembly (1975), critics say that WCC pronouncements chastise Western democratic states and their less-than-democratic allies for their relatively small sins while virtually ignoring the massive violation of nearly all rights under Communist totalitarian regimes.

Responding to this criticism, WCC spokesmen point out that frequent condemnations of the Soviet Union and its European satellites would jeopardize member churches in those countries, or at least limit their participation in the ecumenical movement. Some WCC officers invoke a kind of double standard, insisting that South Africa, for example, which claims to be Christian, should be judged more harshly than East Germany, which is officially atheistic. Forced by criticism and its own conscience, however, the WCC has occasionally spoken against Soviet aggression and imperialism.

The WCC has not completely ignored rights violations in non-aligned Third World states. WCC executives rebuked Idi Amin of Uganda, but no WCC body formally condemned his genocide. The Central Committee did, however, deplore "the fratricidal acts" that left perhaps 10,000 Tutsi and 100,000 Hutu (estimates vary widely) dead in Burundi in 1972-73. The WCC also publicized the facts about the brutal Nguema regime in Equatorial Guinea. Generally, its selective outrage was directed less at oppressive black or left-wing regimes than at authoritarian regimes in Asia and Latin America, which often showed more respect for human rights.

People's Republic of China

Communist China has been a special problem for the WCC. It is a totalitarian state, it claims to be a model for Third World political and economic development, and it does not permit any of its indigenous or mission-founded churches to participate in ecumenical activities. Four Chinese churches were founding members of the WCC in 1948, a year before the Communists conquered the mainland. Their names still appear on the roster, but they have been unable to take part since the Korean War, which began in 1950. The single exception is Anglican bishop K. H. Ting of Nanking, who was permitted to attend a Central Committee meeting in Hungary in 1956.

The World Council has said little about the Chinese Christians who survived the Cultural Revolution. Public contact was reestablished with K. H. Ting, no longer called a bishop, in the early 1970s. Ting is today perhaps the most articulate interpreter of Chinese Christian cooperation with the revolution. It was necessary, he says, to strip the church in China of the vestiges of Western cultural imperialism, to give it genuine Chinese roots. In any event, Christianity in China has been virtually obliterated. Ting and a few others have been allowed to resurface publicly as Christians, but there are no institutional manifestations of the church.

Other than repeatedly advocating U.N. membership for the People's Republic, the WCC has said little about China. Its Commission of the Churches on International Affairs condemned Peking's seizure of Tibet in 1950 and in the mid-1950s consulted with the U.S. State Department on ways to keep the offshore islands of Quemoy and Matsu from being "a thorn in the side of peace." WCC officers sent a message of concern to Indian church leaders in 1962, when Chinese troops occupied the Ladakh region of India.

The Nairobi Assembly (1975) criticized the Peking regime after a long debate. The final resolution said that "whenever human rights are suppressed or violated by any Asian government, churches have a duty to work for the defense of human rights especially of the oppressed."[10] Churches were also urged "to work for the right of the people of Asia to participate in their own development." The resolution mentioned "one-party states in such countries as the People's Republic of China" and added: "In all other countries of Asia (e.g., Malaysia, Singapore, Australasia, New Zealand, Indonesia, and Japan) there are also violations of human rights."[11] Though several kinds of regimes are named, the statement overlooks the profound difference between authoritarian and totalitarian states in terms of the human rights they respect and the quality of life they permit or make possible. From this perspective, authoritarian South Korea is a land of freedom compared with Communist North Korea.

Maoist thought and practice have been much studied in ecumenical circles, both WCC and Roman Catholic, for clues to the impact of revolution on a people. The WCC has published or reprinted numerous articles on contemporary China. While tone and views vary, most of these publications see positive benefits to the Chinese people from the revolution; some compare the Long March to the Exodus of the Israelites and even treat the People's Republic as a new heaven on earth. Disagreements exist on whether China's model of development can be exported.

Nairobi Assembly (1975): Liberation Theology

Originally scheduled for Jakarta, Indonesia, the fifth WCC Assembly was shifted to Nairobi, Kenya, because of conflict between Indonesia's Muslim and Christian communities. Its theme, "Jesus Christ Frees and Unites," reflected the hope for a new ecumenical internationalism. It was the first Assembly south of the equator and the first at which delegate quotas were used for women, the young, and laymen. Of 676 voting delegates, 152 were women, 62 were under thirty, 287 were laymen. (However, Nairobi had 42 per cent clergy while Uppsala had had only 25 per cent clergy.) The geographical breakdown of the delegates was 147 Western Europeans, 137 North Americans, 107 Africans, 97 Eastern Europeans, 92 Asians, 42 from Australasia and the Pacific, 21 Latin Americans, 20 Middle Easterners, and 9 from the Caribbean. Eighty per cent had never attended a WCC Assembly before.

By 1975 dynamic change and revolution were at the top of the WCC agenda. Evangelism and mission had been rebaptized as "liberation" at the 1973 "Salvation Today" conference in Bangkok. The Faith and Order Commission, the WCC's bastion of theological concern, underwent a significant change between its 1971 meeting in Louvain, Belgium, and its 1974 gathering in Accra, Ghana—a change that a Central Committee report described in this way:

Louvain . . . might be characterized as "White theology" at its best. Accra . . . may be seen as marking the transition from "White theology" to "colorful theology"—a theology infused with the contributions of the whole spectrum of cultures, races, and communities. The Accra meeting proved to be a real encounter . . . with the aspirations, fears, and hopes of the Third World.[12]

The mood of the Nairobi Assembly was sounded in a keynote address by Robert McAfee Brown, an American professor of Christian ethics. Brown said he was ashamed of the evil his country had done "and continues to do, to so many of your countries," adding that many persons in the Third World were starving because "American business exploits them."[13] Brown felt so guilty about America's sins that he delivered his address in Spanish to avoid the language of "imperialism."[14]

This exercise in self-flagellation set the stage for the concept of "consciousness-raising," which came into its own at Nairobi. The term "conscientization" was originally popularized by Paulo Freire in Brazil and referred to a way of teaching adults to read and write quickly by using materials from everyday life. It linked the goal of literacy with the improvement of their social, political, and economic conditions. In the late sixties, Freire's word and process were seized upon by liberation advocates. The concept was soon expanded to become a method of teaching oppressed peoples (women, racial minorities, young people, homosexuals, workers, Third World citizens) to understand the causes of their oppression and thus motivating them to improve their lot. Consciousness-raising, said a Central Committee report for Nairobi, attacks "the problem of apathy, the state of human beings who have been so conditioned by their relationships in society that they internalize failure and accept their situations without hoping to change them."[15]

In view of Uppsala's emphasis on self-determination, the WCC's adoption of Freire's doctrine is somewhat ironic. "Conscientization," as Peter Berger has pointed out, is based on the assumption that the oppressed do not understand their own situation and must be enlightened by those of higher consciousness, typically a vanguard of ideologists and intellectuals who "have usually passed through a long period of formal education, and usually come from the upper middle or upper classes of their societies."[16] Uppsala had heard the cries of the exploited, but now the WCC was calling upon the churches to "raise the consciousness" of peoples too apathetic to cry out.

As the central theme at Nairobi, "liberation" was addressed in each of the six sections: (1) Confessing Christ Today, (2) What Unity Requires, (3) Seeking Community—The Common Search of People of Various Faiths, Cultures and Ideologies, (4) Education for Liberation and Community, (5) Structures of Injustice and Struggles for Liberation, and (6) Human Development—The Ambiguities of Power, Technology and Quality of Life. The first two, striking Faith and Order notes, were to investigate the theological and ecclesiastical bases for liberation; the other four dealt with more practical matters.

In contrast to Uppsala, whose delegates had received advance drafts of section reports and commentaries on them, Nairobi had as preparatory materials certain articles and statements selected by WCC staff. This strategy was severely criticized in a seven-page response from the Orthodox Theological Society of America. The papers, it said, showed "almost total neglect of Christian faith and Christian experience—indeed Christ himself—in the ways that problems are selected, rated, categorized and treated."[17] It added:

> In these documents the evils of Western Christian, or post-Christian, societies are severely and relentlessly exposed and criticized. Although many of us question the accuracy and value of such unqualified condemnations of the West, we all agree that there are grounds for a thorough Christian critique of western social, political and economic systems and practices. What we do not accept and must denounce, however, is the absence, in all the preparatory materials, of even the slightest criticism of the human repression perpetrated in the Marxist systems in eastern Europe and elsewhere. Nor is there criticism of the political excesses, violence and curtailment of human liberties in certain nations of the so-called "Third World."[18]

At Nairobi, everything Western and most things Northern were suspect, while the awakened Southern Hemisphere—with the exception, of course, of any Third World regime allegedly kept in power by Western political or economic interests—was viewed in a romantic and revolutionary light. Nothing positive was found in the American or Western democratic systems. This negative view was vigorously advanced in the section report dealing with the "ambiguities of power," adopted with only one dissenting vote (that of a United Presbyterian U.S.A. delegate). The report said, "When liberal democracies" can no longer guarantee profits for the "privileged" from their domestic markets, the privileged turn to "totalitarian regimes" in the Third World, where "torture and terror have become the usual means of government." "International capital" does not hesitate to engage in "subversion" and "political intervention" to consolidate its economic "hegemony."[19] These words could have been copied from a Marxist manual published in Moscow.

Nairobi's favor was reserved for socialist states and the "liberation" movements—with one ironic exception. Canon Burgess Carr, general secretary of the All Africa Conference of Churches, who before Nairobi had said that God has "sanctified violence into a redemptive instrument,"[20] also reminded the delegates at Nairobi of the brutal and undemocratic black regimes in Africa and exclaimed in despair: "But who will deliver us from the black messiahs!"[21]

The revolutionary rhetoric at Nairobi from Professor Brown and others evoked little rebuttal from Western Protestant ecumenical delegates. As guilt-ridden heirs of Christian missions and Western colonialism who lived in affluent societies, they apparently felt they dare not challenge the prevailing Third World outlook, which they, after all, had helped to shape.

The efforts to subject "liberation" to critical theological analysis at Nairobi bore little fruit, in part because the concept meant different things to different persons. Just as the pioneer American prophet of the social gospel, Walter Rauschenbusch, constructed a "theology for the social gospel" after the fact of the late-nineteenth-century liberal social movement,[22] so "liberation theology" followed in the footsteps of the largely secular, and often Marxist, political and social liberation movements of the post–World War II period. Nairobi tried to *forge* and at the same time *apply* a gospel of liberation, an impossible task. The WCC's "liberation theology" was then and is now the confused child of theologians and churchmen of all races who have sought to raise the social consciousness of non-revolutionary Christians—i.e., to persuade them to accept the liberationists' diagnosis and prescriptions if they are to be saved.

In essence, Nairobi proclaimed that poverty, racism, violations of human rights, and militarism (excluding military action by "liberation" groups) the world over result from unjust systems foisted upon humanity by the white-dominated consumer societies of the Northern Hemispere. "Liberation" meant changing or overthrowing unjust structures and replacing them with systems that serve rather than exploit people. Fundamental human rights included "the right to work, to adequate food, to guaranteed health care, to decent housing, and to education for the full development of the human potential."[23] The civil and political rights spelled out in the

U.N. declarations and covenants "largely coincide" with the Christian understanding of a just society, said Nairobi, but they may have no meaning unless they are matched with social and economic "rights."

Nairobi condemned racism in southern Africa, particularly South Africa, and blamed the "white North Atlantic nations" for "trade patterns and preferences that militate against other racial groups."[24] The plights of the Korean minority in Japan, native peoples in North and South America, aboriginal peoples in Australia, ethnic minorities in New Zealand, and black people and migrant workers in Europe were mentioned. In Latin America two countries were named: Argentina was asked to normalize the situation of political refugees and exiles, and Chile was asked to permit the return of ousted Lutheran bishop Helmut Frenz, who had aided refugees and "political prisoners" after the overthrow of Chile's Marxist president Salvador Allende. A proposal to cite human-rights violations in Brazil was withdrawn after clergy from Brazil said this would cause problems for churches and individual Christians at home.

Nairobi failed to rebuke the Soviet Union for its denial of religious liberty, to say nothing of its massive violation of other rights. After a discussion of the 1975 Helsinki Agreement, which called on all parties to guarantee a wide range of rights, efforts to mention the Soviet Union were defeated. Instead, the Assembly asked that religious liberty be "the subject of intensive consultations with the member churches of the signatory states of the Helsinki Agreement."[25] In a novel move, the resolution noted that the Assembly had "devoted a substantial period to the discussion of the alleged denials of religious liberty in the U.S.S.R."[26]

The churches under atheistic, Marxist governments were found to be rediscovering the sources of faith and responding to their situation, which guaranteed few or no rights. African socialism, it was said, was helping many Christians to overcome the Western division between "good and bad ideologies." In Asia, "repressive, technocratic states based on Western capitalism are confronted by varying forms of ideologies advocating human rights, social justice, and people's participation."[27]

Transnational Corporations

At Nairobi, Western technology was no longer seen as an unambiguous economic boon to the Third World. The energy crisis, the environmental movement, and the "limits to growth" philosophy convinced the WCC that the products of science must henceforth be simple in design, be easily maintained, have a less damaging effect on the environment, and be compatible with indigenous materials and culture.

Having earlier urged governments and private enterprise in industrialized countries to transfer capital and technology to the Third World, the WCC at Nairobi took a skeptical if not critical view of this approach. Such transfers, it said, advance the hegemony of the economically powerful few over the destiny of the many weak. The major culprit was the Western transnational corporation:

> These corporations claim to bring capital and technology to the countries where they operate and thereby to create employment and income. But, essentially, their aim is to take advantage of the cheap labor that is available in the host countries and to draw out profits from them, making use of the immense control they exercise over world trade and prices. It must be mentioned that their operations in the poorer countries are with the approval of national governments and often in active collaboration with local private business enterprises. But the type of goods they produce is meant invariably to satisfy the needs of an elite class, the technology they use is ill-suited for the needs of these countries, and the employment they create and the incomes they generate are only to the advantage of the higher income groups in the host countries.[28]

The Uppsala Assembly (1968) had initiated a study of WCC investments, meager though they were, in Western corporations and banks doing business with or in South Africa, and the WCC had sold its holdings in enterprises considered supportive of apartheid. It encouraged member churches to do the same. Some American denominations resisted this approach, deciding rather to use their proxy power as shareholders to oppose apartheid and foster "corporate responsibility." At Nairobi the WCC authorized a critical investigation of transnational corporations. A prime objective was to find better ways of "organizing the earth's resources and human skills."

A critical investigation of transnationals has been a major preoccupation of the WCC in the late 1970s. One of the first reports on a specific situation appeared in the March 1978 *One World*, the WCC monthly. According to data provided by an Anglican bishop in Kenya, transnational soap subsidiaries in that country were driving locally owned manufacturers out of business through mechanization and advertising, huge profits were being taken out of the country, and soap advertising was helping to turn Kenya "into a Western-style consumer society."[29] Moreover, the transnationals were paying African managers at North American and European levels, which created a local managerial class and inflated local salaries. This report seemed oddly inconsistent: the ecumenical world for years has insisted that companies in South Africa promote blacks to the managerial levels and pay them on a par with whites. (In August 1977, the Central Committee called for a complete international embargo against South Africa and urged shareholder actions against oil companies making sales to Rhodesia.)

Nairobi's virulent attack on the West, and especially on the United States, its condemnation of "capitalism," its virtual silence on human-rights violations in Communist countries, its ill-defined and romantic view of "liberation," and its lopsided critique of constitutional democracy—all this had an ironic twist. Here was a diverse, hymn-singing assembly asserting its unity, yet behaving in a very Western way: issuing protest proclamations Western-style at a conference organized on a Western model sponsored by an organization created in the West and supported largely by Western money. Few of the North Americans and Western Europeans, still the largest cultural bloc in the WCC, seemed to sense the irony. Chafing under a self-imposed burden of guilt, they were too busy leading the protesters in denouncing the sins of their own Western societies. The Nairobi Assembly ended where it began—in the mood of Western self-flagellation symbolized by Brown's breast-beating address.

Since 1975, the WCC has followed the course charted at Nairobi. In some respects it has managed to soften the strident rhetoric, but in others it has become even more revolutionary. At the same time, the more conservative Orthodox member churches have found a new visibility in the WCC journal *One World*, which may suggest that the Council is giving closer attention to the Faith and Order concerns of the ecumenical movement. The Faith and Order Commission, which celebrated its fiftieth anniversary in 1977, is working toward a theological consensus on baptism, the eucharist, and the ministry. There is a new emphasis on evangelism and on worship. But as the Jamaica meeting of the Central Committee in January 1979 demonstrated, liberation theology—symbolized by the support of Marxist-oriented guerrilla forces—is still in the WCC saddle.

CHAPTER FIVE

Ends, Means, and Consequences

Christianity has an extraordinary propensity to regard its own replacements with benign approval.

EDWARD NORMAN[1]

DURING THE LONG ROAD from Amsterdam in 1948 through Nairobi in 1975 to the present, the World Council of Churches has shown an increasing interest in the problems and demands of the Third World, both as a geographical entity and as a symbol of political, economic, and cultural repression. In word and deed, the Council—its Geneva staff, its presidents, its Central Committee and Executive Committee, its five Assemblies, and its special Church and Society conferences—has moved from a largely Western concept of political responsibility to a more radical ideology that by 1975 embraced the concept and practice of "liberation theology."

In its early years the WCC advocated creating "the responsible society" by peaceful, democratic, and constitutional means. Gradually this gave way to a qualified approval of violent and revolutionary change in the Third World, and in several cases even support for terrorist groups. Western political norms were replaced, at least in part, by an ideology that laid the chief blame for the ills of the Third World on the sins of the West, particularly the United States—its foreign policy and its transnational corporations. At the 1966 Geneva Conference on Church and Society, WCC thinking on "rapid social change" was transformed into a revolutionary doctrine that became most dramatically evident in the Program to Combat Racism.

The more radical stance both reflected and nourished the prevailing Third World outlook, which was developed largely by liberal and Marxist

47

intellectuals in the West and exported to Asia, Africa, and Latin America by "liberation" missionaries, by returning students who had studied in the West, and by ecumenical conferences. This outlook was, as Daniel Patrick Moynihan has pointed out, in part a product of British and French socialist thought, which stressed economic distribution rather than production and was persistently anti-American.[2] Its American manifestation has been documented by a score of scholars, including Peter L. Berger[3] and Richard John Neuhaus.[4] As P. T. Bauer has pointed out, the Western revolutionary worldview was stimulated in part by a widespread sense of guilt among American intellectuals rooted in the domestic racial situation, America's wealth, and U.S. involvement in Vietnam.[5]

The "liberation theology" that emerged from the Nairobi Assembly was largely an elite phenomenon, a product of the university, though it sought to deal with the problems of poverty, injustice, and oppression in Asia, Africa, and Latin America. The WCC's interest in liberation was rooted in Christian compassion, but its stance was influenced more by current secular sources than by the traditional social teachings of Christianity. The emergence of liberation theology bears out the observation of the late Pope Paul VI: noting the church's "loss of confidence in the great masters of Christian thought," Paul said the vacuum has "all too often been filled by a superficial and almost servile acceptance of the currently fashionable philosophies."[6] In the same vein, Edward Norman, an Anglican priest who is a professor at Cambridge University, said that Christianity today has "increasingly borrowed its political outlook and vocabulary, the issues it regards as most urgently requiring attention, and even its tests of moral virtue, from the progressive thinking of the surrounding secular culture,"[7] not from the classical Christian tradition of St. Augustine, St. Thomas, Martin Luther, or John Calvin. Radical Christians of the Third World persuasion "are not the wretched of the earth," he says, but "members of the bourgeois elite, emotionally attached to the idealism of social change. Their radicalism is itself a class characteristic of disaffected elements within the intelligentsia."[8]

The Marxist Connection

In its fervor and utopian character, this Third World ideology with its call "to make all things new" bears a striking resemblance to the most powerful secular utopianism of our time, Marxism. Christianity and Marxism address the same perennial questions, often use similar language, but affirm profoundly different interpretations of man and history and of the cause and cure of the world's ills. However, the mood of the Nairobi Assembly was such that Friedrich Engels's words, "Everything that exists deserves to perish," had they been uttered by Robert McAfee Brown, might well have been applauded by the liberationists, who called for an end to what they regarded as the structural flaws of the West—materialism, consumerism, neo-imperialism, repression, and exploitation by transnational corporations.

In diagnosis and prescription, the WCC's liberation theology is strikingly similar to current Marxist concepts. The positions the WCC has taken in some controversial situations have been indistinguishable from those taken in Moscow or Havana. The most dramatic example is the "humanitarian" grants to the two Marxist-led guerrilla groups in the latter part of 1978: $85,000 to the so-called Patriotic Front, which was seeking to shoot its way into power in Rhodesia, and $125,000 to SWAPO, which was fighting toward the same objective in South West Africa—both against interim interracial regimes. There were three reasons for this concurrence in the perspectives of the WCC and the Marxists: (1) The WCC's almost obsessive concern with "white racism," or what was perceived as such, tended to blind it to all other factors in the situation. (2) The WCC leaders tended to find Marxist "solutions" to "racism" more convincing than peaceful, constitutional, and democratic approaches. (3) WCC leaders persisted in seeing a radically changed racial-political situation in obsolete and nonfactual terms. Hence, the Rhodesian and South West African cases in 1978 are full of irony: the issue was no longer race or racism but rather how power was to be transferred and what policies the new majority regime was likely to pursue. In the real world the net effect of these WCC grants was to support guerrillas who sought to install by terror a minority authoritarian regime against the parties that were vying for power by democratic and constitutional means, parties committed to a one-man–one-vote, non-racial, multi-party state with a separation of power among the executive, legislative, and judicial branches.

Another point of concurrence between the WCC and the Marxists was Vietnam. The WCC's Geneva Conference said U.S. military action to defend South Vietnam against aggression from the North "cannot be justified" but was only mildly critical of that aggression itself, which it called "the military infiltration of the South by the North."

The concurrence of the WCC and the Marxists on certain Third World issues does not mean that the WCC leaders were Marxists. It does suggest, however, that these leaders found Marxist analyses of the cause and cure of such problems more attractive than the more gradual, democratic, and peaceful approaches. One reason for this is the dogged determination of many religious leaders in an increasingly secular society to seek to recapture moral authority, if not headlines, by running with the radical-chic pack—which usually takes its cue from the hard Left on political issues. Trendy clergymen and laymen are often engaged in a thinly disguised rivalry with secular revolutionaries for "relevance."

The Jamaica meeting of the Central Committee in January 1979, which endorsed the WCC grants to the two guerrilla groups, makes it clear that the concept and practice of liberation theology has prevailed in the inner circles of the Council. But the debate before, during, and after this meeting shows that the issue is far from settled. For years there has been a growing backlash against the radicalization of the WCC. This has been expressed in verbal protest and also in the withholding of contributions not only to the WCC's social-action efforts but to the ecumenical movement in general. (The WCC, which receives about three-fourths of its income from U.S. and West German churches, anticipates a deficit of $2.8 million in 1979, largely because of the drop in the value of the dollar and mark against the Swiss franc. U.S. churches now donate about one-third of the Council's budget, down from four-fifths of the budget twenty years ago.)

The wellspring of WCC radicalism may be the Geneva headquarters staff, though vigorous streams flow through the larger ecumenical and denominational social-action establishment. Dwain C. Epps of the Geneva staff reportedly said WCC officials admit that the staff are "nearly all socialists."[9] This does not mean, of course, that they are Marxists (though there have been, says Richard John Neuhaus, a few WCC officials who "proclaim their commitment to Marxist socialism, to Mao's rediscovery of primitive Christianity, and the like"[10]). It does suggest, however, a strong influence of Marxist thought at the core of the World Council.

The double standard sometimes found in WCC pronouncements on repression or human rights suggests an apologetic posture toward, if not an affinity for, socialist and Marxist rather than democratic and non-socialist regimes in the Third World. In the last decade or so, WCC spokesmen have often protested alleged violations of human and political rights in the Western democracies and allied nations, while remaining strangely silent about more grievous violations in Marxist states or in Third World countries that embrace, at least in part, the Marxist model.

There is ample evidence for concern about the deep and widespread impact of the Marxist interpretation of history and strategy for change within WCC circles and among liberal Christians generally. Professor Norman correctly notes:

> One of the most striking developments of the last twenty years has been the way in which all the Churches—Catholic, Orthodox, Protestant—have responded in about the same degree to the secular political ideologies. There are, in consequence, for the first time in history, no enormous differences in the social priorities of the major Churches. The only significant modification to this is the difference of emphasis imposed by the division between those who have adapted to the Marxist socialism of the eastern European bloc, and those who have absorbed the liberal social radicalism, with all its Marxist rhetoric, of the west and of the developing world. The Vatican, with its authoritative background of social teachings, and its diplomatic professionalism, is the most restrained and generalized in its pronouncements, though these are plainly reformist in tone and intention. . . . It is the organization of the Protestants and the Orthodox, the World Council of Churches, that most specifically engages in the detailed application of contemporary political doctrines.[11]

Norman fears that this embrace of Marxist socialism or liberal radicalism— each of which involves a far-reaching criticism of Western values—is preparing the ground for the success of Marxism in the Third World.

Confusion of Ends and Means

The ambiguity toward Marxism—a mixture of infatuation and fear— that characterizes the Third World ideology is evident in both secular and Christian circles in the West. This ambiguity stems from a profound confusion between ends and means—the ends of justice, freedom, order, and plenty and the appropriate means for achieving these goals, or at least moving toward them. The Marxists have a clear-cut diagnosis and simple answers. They play upon Western feelings of guilt. These feelings are especially strong among upper-middle-class intellectuals and idealists— and it is mainly persons of this sort who founded and still shape the WCC.

Christianity offers no simple cure for poverty, injustice, or lack of freedom. And so Christians who are rightly concerned about the world's ills are often confused about how to mitigate them. Many Western Christians, feeling guilty that they are rich while most of the rest of the world is poor, are prone to exaggerate the sins of their own society and play down the greater evils of the Marxist solution. Looking at the vast problems in the Third World, they are sometimes beguiled by the totalitarian temptation— the acceptance of a temporary tyranny to impose order and justice on poor, confused, and often unwilling people. The democratic and peaceful way seems too slow, undramatic, and unfashionable.

The liberation theologians also underestimate the values of a market economy over a Marxist or socialist economy. They have refused to accept the fact that market economies with minimal government restrictions have demonstrated a far greater capacity to produce and distribute goods and services than Marxist and other government-controlled economies. They tend to accept the neo-Marxist myth that colonialism, neo-colonialism, and transnational corporations are the causes of poverty in the Third World. Marx and Engels did not share this view. They acknowledged that these Western forces enhanced the material well-being of Third World peoples, though they insisted rightly that the distribution of goods and services in traditional societies was unjust. Poverty is the plight of all primitive or traditional peoples; not until the rise of industrial capitalism did any society have the capacity to eliminate stark poverty. Ironically, industrial capitalism, which owes so much to the Protestant work ethic, has now become the favorite whipping boy of the liberation theologians.

Political and economic development in the Third World is difficult in the best of circumstances, and circumstances do vary widely; but empirical evidence suggests that both prosperity and respect for human rights are more likely to result from adapting local conditions to a Western, democratic, market model than from following the rigid and harsh Marxist models of the Soviet Union, Cuba, or Angola. The quality of economic, political, and cultural life possible, to say nothing of the respect for religious freedom, is far greater in Taiwan than in Communist China, in South Korea than in North Korea, in Singapore than in Burma. The United States, Western Europe, and Japan have demonstrated that political, economic, and religious freedom reinforce one another. None of these societies has solved or is likely to solve all its problems. But certainly the level of material and cultural life possible is significantly greater under industrial capitalism than in any known Marxist society. It is to the advantage of any Third World state to engage in mutually beneficial trade and investment with Western democratic states and to emulate as far as feasible the human-rights achievements of these states.

The Separate Spheres of Church and State

The World Council's efforts on behalf of the Third World have suffered because of confusion over the relation between the City of God and the City of Man, between church and state, between the Christian as a child of God and the Christian as a citizen. These are perplexing relationships that cannot be defined with precision. The Christian faith is concerned with both time and eternity. The church is not the state, and few Christian citizens are statesmen.

The functions of the church and the state are complementary. Representing the City of God, the church serves as the conscience of society, the custodian of its highest values. The state—like the church an institution ordained by God—protects the people within its territory and administers a system of justice. The church upholds the values of justice, security, and liberty; the responsible state secures and protects these values. The church speaks out against cruelty, injustice, repression, slavery, tyranny, and genocide; the responsible state, with the support of conscientious citizens, develops policies and instruments to fight these evils.

In our time the proper roles of church and state, politics and religion, have been blurred and confused, to the detriment of both institutions and of society itself. The Second Vatican Council rightly declared: "The Church is quite distinct from the political community and uncommitted to any political system; she is at once the sign and the guarantee that human personality transcends the field of politics."[12] It is morally wrong and politically unwise for the church to identify itself or Christianity with any political cause, movement, party, or regime. The principal spiritual danger is that of absolutizing a relative policy or santifying a contingent cause. All such worldly efforts—however necessary—embrace both good and evil elements. Identification deprives the church of the critical distance essential for judging the behavior of any human institution or program in the light of eternal and universal principles. This is why mainstream Protestantism, as well as contemporary Catholicism, opposes the theocratic state, in which temporal power and ecclesiastical authority are too closely identified. The same Protestant tradition also opposes so-called Christian democratic or Christian socialist parties.

In contrast to the essential aloofness of the churches rooted in transcendent values, individual Christians as citizens can and should participate in partisan political causes, supporting those that show some promise of advancing justice, freedom, or order.

In both the more distant and the recent past, some Christians and secularists have sought to identify political causes with the Christian mission. In 1846, Richard Cobden said the repeal of the Corn Laws in England was "the most important event in history since the coming of Christ."[13] In 1928, the U.S. Methodist Church in the South declared that the Kellogg-Briand Pact to outlaw war was "shot through with the light that shone in Bethlehem."[14] More recently, Fidel Castro said "Christ was a great revolutionary," adding that he saw no incompatibility between Christianity and Cuban socialism.[15] Dr. Philip Potter, general secretary of the WCC, once said that it "has been the secular writers and politicians who have been the prophets of our time," and that the Black Power leaders Stokeley Carmichael and Malcolm X "have given far more clear and powerful expression to the true meaning of the right hand of God than the Churches."[16]

Such assertions, however unfortunate and ill-conceived, are relatively harmless. Far more dangerous is the WCC's identification with the Marxist terrorists who were attempting to shoot their way into power in Rhodesia and South West Africa and to impose an elitest, Communist-style "revolutionary state" (to use the words of Robert Mugabe, leader of the more radical wing of the Rhodesian guerrillas). Taking sides and not taking sides both have moral and political pitfalls. But supporting the wrong side is the worst of all options.

The churches as churches should take no sides in armed power struggles in Rhodesia or elsewhere. Governments and Christians as citizens should support what they believe to be right and in their interests. If the WCC insists on supporting terrorists over an interracial coalition seeking power by peaceful means, it should not do so in the name of humanitarian aid. That is a sham. Refugees on both sides of the Rhodesian border needed help, and any aid to the political force on either side would enable it to divert more resources to the fighting. Further, the WCC had no way of ascertaining how the guerrillas would use the funds, and it made no provision for monitoring their use. Nor did it channel the grant through a respected impartial agency like the International Red Cross—because, according to one WCC official, this would have implied that the WCC did not trust the guerrillas.[17]

The WCC's Central Committee should have been honest with itself, its member churches, and the world by invoking the Christian concept of the just war to explain the moral basis of its grants. In fact, that was precisely what it was doing, but it lacked the courage or candor to say so. Had it done so it would have undercut the charges of hypocrisy and double-talk and earned respect for an honest explanation of its direct involvement in a political power struggle. But it would also have faced the herculean task of documenting what made revolutionary terrorism just.

The consequences of the Rhodesian and SWAPO grants are likely to be unfortunate both for the cause of Christian unity and for the cause of justice and freedom in the world. For the churches, the grants revealed once more a profound confusion between the separate responsibilities of church and state. This has sown the seeds of division within the WCC and beyond, and it gives the lie to the old Life and Work slogan, "Doctrine divides, service unites." Commenting on the Central Committee's endorsement of the guerrilla grants, the French Canadian priest J. M. R. Tillard said: "The walls of mutual incomprehension are tumbling down" but "the involvement of Christians in the world's problems and their identification with the aspirations of their peoples are raising new walls."[18]

While the outcome of the Rhodesian struggle is not clear at this writing, it may be that the WCC's support of the guerrillas will be just enough to tip the scales in their favor, thus frustrating a peaceful and constitutional effort that would have had a real chance of establishing the first multiracial and democratic state on the continent of Africa. But regardless of the impact of the WCC grants in southern Africa, we can conclude that the Council's flirtation with the totalitarian temptation and its misguided theology of liberation have struck a blow against peaceful change and human rights.

Concluding Observations

There are several measures that would help the World Council of Churches and its constituent denominations make a more responsible political witness in our troubled world:

1. First, and perhaps most important, the WCC should ponder more deeply the long theological and ethical heritage of its Protestant and Orthodox member churches—a heritage that draws upon the Old Testament prophets, the teachings of Jesus, and the writings of the great theologians, from St. Paul, St. Augustine, and St. Thomas, through the reformers John Calvin and Martin Luther, down to the modern interpreters of this tradition. The rich body of Christian social teaching needs to be studied, refined, and updated. In "leapfrogging from one problem to another," says Paul Ramsey, the WCC has been escaping the difficult task of rebuilding a "disintegrated" social ethic.[19] Among other things, this rebuilding would mean a renewed emphasis on the Faith and Order mission of the WCC and a more vigorous dialogue between the Faith and Order movement and the Church and Society movement.

2. The churches have frequently acted with superficial knowledge and with little understanding of either political theory or the dynamics of social structures. Ecumenical leaders should make fuller use of the research and analysis of social, political, and economic issues generated by universities and public-policy research centers. This information on questions as different as nuclear deterrence, land use, and economic productivity varies in quality and perspective, but when wisely used it can provide a much better understanding of issues addressed by the churches. Not only would it be vastly more trustworthy than the ideological slogans of the extreme left or right, but it would help to distinguish what should be preserved, what should be improved, and the best means of accomplishing the desired objectives. This kind of insight, rooted in empirical analysis, would help to separate the specific, technical issues on which the churches should not comment from the broader issues that merit their serious attention. Churches cannot be and should not strive to be competent in scores of complex economic and political issues that only specialists and large agencies are capable of handling. Their realm of competence is moral judgment. As Paul H. Nitze, a former U.S. deputy secretary of defense, said:

> When our political leaders look to the public for guidance on tactical issues, or even on matters of strategy, they err and are delinquent in their duty. When they ignore the essential values of the people in deciding specific tactics, they err more seriously.[20]

3. The WCC should develop a clearer understanding of the different but complementary functions of church, state, and citizen. The church is the conscience not only of the state but of society as a whole. Hence the church can speak to the total contemporary situation—the family, the school, the economy, the arts, the culture, and the government—by making broad moral judgments but not by giving specific advice better left to individual Christians and other citizens working in these institutions. As consumers, parents, citizens, and participants in a thousand different vocations, Christians play a direct part in influencing the course of a society and the policies of its government. The word becomes flesh not through church pronouncements but through the daily acts of fidelity on the part of millions of Christians going about their work, whether it be that of a telephone operator, a teacher, an economist, a farmer, a congressman, or the president of the United States.

4. The World Council should use more fully the rich diversity of traditions and gifts within its ranks. The Geneva staff has suffered from too much ideological homogeneity. Church and Society activities, including the Program to Combat Racism, have been run largely by a self-perpetuating elite (including the WCC social-action staff and denominational officers concerned chiefly with social issues) who have been heavily influenced by the radical liberation approach to the Third World. There has been some diversity, but far too little. An effort should be made to recruit a headquarters staff more varied in theological, ethical, and political outlook. The social-action establishment has often been more eager to talk to Marxists than to conservative evangelical Christians. This is a sad irony. Also largely excluded from inner WCC circles are persons who have special knowledge or skills on matters with which the WCC is occupied but whose ideology deviates too far from the current ecumenical fashion.

5. One way of increasing the diversity of the WCC in the Church and Society area is for the Council and its constituent churches to become more democratic, more reflective of the millions of Christians they represent. Most Protestants believe in the "priesthood of all believers," which means that clergy and laymen have equal responsibility for the Christian mission. Therefore, church councils would have much to gain by bringing in, or at least taking into account, laymen from all walks of life and all political persuasions. It will be argued that this would reduce all social pronouncements to a bland, lowest-common-denominator level and that their prophetic cutting edge would be blunted. There is indeed a difference between a prophetic witness and a nose-counting consensus. Pronouncements certainly should not be made on the basis of a public-opinion poll. They should emerge from long and hard study fortified by the testimony of experts and experienced persons; but they should not ignore the values and insights of the mass of church members, as some of them have conspicuously done. If politicians benefit from consulting the man in the street, ecumenical leaders would likewise benefit from consulting the man in the pew. Politicians, unlike intellectuals, cannot afford to be elitests.

The problem is complicated by an organizational fact. Cynthia Wedel, one of the WCC presidents, laments that "half the member churches cannot be represented even in the Central Committee, and many who represent their churches on commissions and committees have no direct access to the decision-making bodies of their own churches."[21] This problem would not be so serious if the Geneva staff and the laymen in the pew were guided by the same ethical norms and committed to the same causes, but, as *Christianity Today* pointed out, if they are "marching to different drummers, the elite can take up a position that, if not arrogant, is highly condescending."[22]

6. The primary obligation of the WCC in the political realm is to speak *to* its member churches, not *for* them. Council and denominational leaders should seek to clarify political and social issues in the light of the Christian ethic and to motivate individuals to be responsible citizens. This is by far the most important task. WCC pronouncements should be more like papal encyclicals, which instruct the faithful in basic moral precepts and relate those precepts to current realities. There are situations of grave danger or great opportunity when the Council may appropriately address pronouncements to secular authorities or other agencies, but these statements should focus on moral judgment rather than on specific policy or tactical advice. In the name of all that Christianity stands for, the churches should raise their voices against genocide, the refusal of a government to permit impartial humanitarian aid to civilian victims of war or natural disaster, and other cases of gross inhumanity. Professor Paul Ramsey of Princeton University states the case well:

> It has been easier to arrive at specific recommendations and condemnations after inadequate deliberation than to penetrate to a deeper and deeper level the meaning of Christian responsibility—leaving to the conscience of individuals and groups of individuals both the task and the freedom to arrive at specific conclusions through untrammeled debate about particular social policies. Radical steps need to be taken in ecumenical ethics if ever we are to correct the pretense that we are makers of political policy and get on with our proper task of nourishing, judging, and repairing the moral and political *ethos* of our

time. . . . Our quest should be to find out whether there is anything especially Christian and especially important that churchmen *as such* may have to say in the public forum concerning the direction of public policy—not directives for it.[23]

7. The WCC should not presume to speak *for* the churches, much less for their millions of members. The Council has neither a theological nor an institutional justification for claiming to represent Christians from 100 countries. Richard John Neuhaus illustrates the problem of whom the WCC represents by referring to the testimony of William Thompson, a member of the WCC Central Committee, before the U.N. Security Council in 1977:

> Some time after bringing greetings "on behalf of the Christian churches of the world," Mr. Thompson said: "I do not presume to speak for the member churches of these ecumenical bodies. . . . I appear today as an individual." Much later, having stated why the South African social system is odious to Christian conscience, he said: "It is my privilege to share something of attitudes which the churches have in this matter." In the end he invoked in support of his view "the position of many churches throughout the world." That position is summarized in the statement that, with respect to South Africa, "*the Christian community* must confront any forces that deny human dignity, equality, freedom or life itself" (emphasis added). One should not blame Mr. Thompson for the confusion about whether he is speaking for, in, or to the Church. It is part of the structural ambiguity of the ecumenical agencies themselves. However, nobody at the U.N. hearing would have received any other impression than that they were listening to a spokesman for the churches, if not for the Church.[24]

Perhaps this confusion over whom the WCC represents is not really that serious, because there is little evidence that church pronouncements either instruct or influence statesmen. If a pronouncement appeals to the conscience of the statesman, it may reinforce his prior disposition. If it is too vague or too specific to be useful, he can ignore it. After all, morally concerned statesmen who from childhood have been instructed by Christian ethics are wise enough to reject foolish advice from the churches precisely because of their loyalty to what the churches fundamentally stand for. Christian men and women in positions of political responsibility are in a far better position to relate the Christian ethic to the perplexing and sometimes tragic realm of political necessity than are professional churchmen, because the statesmen have been disciplined by a deeper sense of history and chastened in the crucible of responsibility.

8. The churches should make the fundamental distinction between a *condition* and a *problem*. This is particularly important in addressing the complex and diverse issues in the Third World. The vast majority of regimes in Asia, Africa, and Latin America are weak, fragile, and poor and are run by authoritarian elites. The range of political and economic choice is very narrow, but great expectations are engendered in these countries by their envy of the West's wealth and power. Ever present is the totalitarian temptation, which seems to offer a short cut to control, modernization, and plenty.

In all Third World countries, including the oil-producing states, expectations far outpace the available material and human resources. This is the *condition* of the Third World. A condition in this sense cannot be changed; it must be faced and endured. Perhaps over time a condition will alter and yield some *problems* that can be at least mitigated, if not solved. This tragic Third World situation is a mirror, perhaps a distorted mirror, of the human situation.

The utopian Marxists and theologians sympathetic to them both have a naïve and stereotyped view of the Third World. They look upon it as malleable, subject to external manipulation, responsive to quick reform or revolutionary transformation. And as we have seen in chapter 4, the liberationists of the West have selected Third World spokesmen who share their romantic vision. Some of the liberation theologians are what Reinhold Niebuhr has called "soft utopians" who believe the brave new world can be brought in by education, development assistance, and other noncoercive means. Others are "hard utopians" who have succumbed to the totalitarian temptation and insist that the new order can be built only after the old is destroyed; they approve or advocate revolutionary violence and the dictatorship of an enlightened elite to achieve their ends. They want to abolish poverty and establish justice by a strong central authority on the Marxist model, which requires the indefinite suppression of human freedom. They reject gradual, peaceful, constructive change based on mutually beneficial political, security, and economic ties with the West, which they regard as decadent. In short, utopians of all stripes refuse to accept the intractable realities of the Third World. The soft utopians have no solution, and the "solution" of the hard utopians is likely to be harsher or more chaotic than the antecedent situation.

The course of wisdom and moral responsibility for the WCC would be to encourage the peaceful and lawful forces that are trying to deal constructively with the problems of poverty, injustice, and lack of freedom. There have been, of course, situations so rigid or dangerous that armed violence was the only responsible option. The strike against Pearl Harbor and North Korea's invasion across the thirty-eighth parallel in 1950 were situations that justified a violent response. Most crises are more ambiguous.

WCC leaders should develop a deeper appreciation for the tenacity of the political, economic, and ethnic problems in the Third World. Only then will the Council's words and deeds speak to the real condition of concerned citizens and statesmen in Asia, Africa, and Latin America who are trying to make a better life. We would all do well to recall the truth of Reinhold Niebuhr's famous prayer: "God, grant me the courage to change what can be changed, the patience to accept what cannot be changed, and the wisdom to know the difference."

APPENDIX A

The Church and the Disorder of Society

A Report from the Amsterdam Assembly of the World Council of Churches, 1948

This report more than any other adopted by the Inaugural Assembly of the WCC deals with social and political issues related to the Third World. It was received by the Assembly and commended to the churches for their "serious consideration and appropriate action." The text is from First Assembly of the World Council of Churches: Amsterdam, Holland, August 22nd–September 4th, 1948 *(Geneva, Switzerland: World Council of Churches, 1948), pages 39-47.*

I. THE DISORDER OF SOCIETY

The world today is experiencing a social crisis of unparalled proportions. The deepest root of that disorder is the refusal of men to see and admit that their responsibility to God stands over and above their loyalty to any earthly community and their obedience to any worldly power. Our modern society, in which religious tradition and family life have been weakened, and which is for the most part secular in its outlook, underestimates both the depth of evil in human nature and the full height of freedom and dignity in the children of God.

The Christian Church approaches the disorder of our society with faith in the Lordship of Jesus Christ. In Him God has established His Kingdom and its gates stand open for all who will enter. Their lives belong to God with a certainty that no disorder of society can destroy, and on them is laid the duty to seek God's Kingdom and His righteousness.

In the light of that Kingdom, with its judgment and mercy, Christians are conscious of the sins which corrupt human communities and institutions in every age, but they are also assured of the final victory over all sin and death through Christ. It is He who has bidden us pray that God's Kingdom may come and His will may be done on earth as it is in heaven; and our obedience to that command requires that we seek in every age to overcome the specific disorders which aggravate the perennial evil in human society, and that we search out the means of securing their elimination or control.

Men are often disillusioned by finding that changes of particular systems do not bring unqualified good, but fresh evils. New temptations to greed and power arise even in systems more just than those they have replaced because sin is ever present in the human heart. Many, therefore, lapse into apathy, irresponsibility and despair. The Christian faith leaves no room for such despair, being based on the fact that the Kingdom of God is firmly established in Christ and will come by God's act despite all human failure.

Two chief factors contribute to the crisis of our age. One of these is the vast concentrations of power—which are under capitalism mainly economic and under communism both economic and political. In such conditions, social evil is manifest on the largest scale not only in the greed, pride, and cruelty of persons and groups; but also in the momentum or inertia of huge organizations of men, which diminish their ability to act as moral and accountable beings. To find ways of realizing personal responsibility for collective action in the large aggregations of power in modern society is a task which has not yet been undertaken seriously.

The second factor is that society, as a whole dominated as it is by technics, is likewise more controlled by a momentum of its own than in previous periods. While it enables men the better to use nature, it has the possibilities of destruction, both through war and through the undermining of the natural foundations of society in family, neighborhood and craft. It has collected men into great industrial cities and has deprived many societies of those forms of association in which men can grow most fully as persons. It has accentuated the tendency in men to waste God's gift to them in the soil and in other natural resources.

On the other hand, technical developments have relieved men and women of much drudgery and poverty, and are still capable of doing more. There is a limit to what they can do in this direction. Large parts of the world, however, are far from that limit. Justice demands that the inhabitants of Asia and Africa, for instance, should have benefits of more machine production. They may learn to avoid the mechanization of life and the other dangers of an unbalanced economy which impair the social health of the older industrial peoples. Technical progress also provides channels of communication and interdependence which can be aids to fellowship, though closer contact may also produce friction.

There is no inescapable necessity for society to succumb to undirected developments of technology, and the Christian Church has an urgent responsibility today to help men to achieve fuller personal life within the technical society.

In doing so, the Churches should not forget to what extent they themselves have contributed to the very evils which they are tempted to blame wholly on the secularism of society. While they have raised up many Christians who have taken the lead in movements of reform, and while many of them have come to see in a fresh way the relevance of their faith to the problems of society, and the imperative obligations thus laid upon them, they share responsibility for the contemporary disorder. Our churches have often given religious sanction to the special privileges of dominant classes, races and political groups, and so they have been obstacles to changes necessary in the interests of social justice and political freedom. They have often concentrated on a purely spiritual or other-worldly or individualistic interpretation of their message and their responsibility. They have often failed to understand the forces which have shaped society around them, and so they have been unprepared to deal creatively with new problems as they have arisen in technical civilization; they have often neglected the effects of industrialization on agricultural communities.

II.   ECONOMIC AND POLITICAL ORGANIZATION

In the industrial revolution economic activity was freed from previous social controls and outgrew its modest place in human life. It created the vast network of financial, commercial and industrial relations which we know as the capitalist order. In all parts of the world new controls have in various degrees been put upon the free play of economic forces, but there are economic necessities which no political system can afford to defy. In our days for instance, the need for stability in the value of money, for creation of capital and for incentives in production, is inescapable and world-wide. Justice, however, demands that economic activities be subordinated to social ends. It is intolerable that vast millions of people be exposed to insecurity, hunger and frustration by periodic inflation or depression.

The Church cannot resolve the debate between those who feel that the primary solution is to socialize the means of production, and those who fear that such a course will merely lead to new and inordinate combinations of political and economic power, culminating finally in an omnicompetent State. In the light of the Christian understanding of man we must, however, say to the advocates of socialization that the institution of property is not the root of the corruption of human nature. We must equally say to the defenders of existing property relations that ownership is not an unconditional right; it must, therefore, be preserved, curtailed or distributed in accordance with the requirements of justice.

On the one hand we must vindicate the supremacy of persons over purely technical considerations by subordinating all economic processes and cherished rights to the needs of the community as a whole. On the other hand, we must preserve the possibility of a satisfying life for "little men in big societies." We must prevent abuse of authority and keep open as wide a sphere as possible in which men can have direct and responsible relations with each other as persons.

Coherent and purposeful ordering of society has now become a major necessity. Here governments have responsibilities which they must not shirk. But centres of initiative in economic life must be so encouraged as to avoid placing too great a burden upon centralized judgment and decision. To achieve religious, cultural, economic, social and other ends it is of vital importance that society should have a rich variety of smaller forms of community, in local government, within industrial organizations, including trade unions, through the development of public corporations and through voluntary associations. By such means it is possible to prevent an undue centralization of power in modern, technically organized communities, and thus escape the perils of tyranny while avoiding the dangers of anarchy.

III.   THE RESPONSIBLE SOCIETY

Man is created and called to be a free being, responsible to God and his neighbour. Any tendencies in State and society depriving man of the possibility of acting responsibly are a denial of God's intention for man and His work of salvation. A responsible society is one where freedom is the freedom of men who acknowledge responsibility to justice and public order, and where those who hold political authority or economic power are responsible for its exercise to God and the people whose welfare is affected by it.

Man must never be made a mere means for political or economic ends. Man is not made for the State but the State for man. Man is not made for production, but production for man. For a society to be responsible under modern conditions it is required that the people have freedom to control, to criticize and to change their governments, that power be made responsible by law and tradition, and be distributed as widely as possible through the whole community. It is required that economic justice and provision of equality of opportunity be established for all the members of society.

We therefore condemn:

1. Any attempt to limit the freedom of the Church to witness to its Lord and His design for mankind and any attempt to impair the freedom of men to obey God and to act according to conscience, for those freedoms are implied in man's responsibility before God;

2. Any denial to man of an opportunity to participate in the shaping of society, for this is a duty implied in man's responsibility towards his neighbour;

3. Any attempt to prevent men from learning and spreading the truth.

IV.   COMMUNISM AND CAPITALISM

Christians should ask why communism in its modern totalitarian form makes so strong an appeal to great masses of people in many parts of the world. They should recognize the hand of God in the revolt of multitudes against injustice that gives communism much of its strength. They should seek to recapture for the Church the original Christian solidarity with the world's distressed people, not to curb their aspirations towards justice, but, on the contrary, to go beyond them and direct them towards the only road which does not lead to a blank wall, obedience to God's will and His justice. Christians should realize that for many, especially for many young men and women, communism seems to stand for a vision of human equality and universal brotherhood for which they were prepared by Christian influences. Christians who are beneficiaries of capitalism should try to see the world as it appears to many who know themselves excluded from its privileges and who see in communism a means of deliverance from poverty and insecurity. All should understand that the proclamation of racial equality by communists and their support of the cause of colonial peoples makes a strong appeal to the populations of Asia and Africa and to racial minorities elsewhere. It is a great human tragedy that so much that is good in the motives and aspirations of many communists and of those whose sympathies they win has been transformed into a force that engenders new forms of injustice and oppression, and that what is true in communist criticism should be used to give convincing power to untrustworthy propaganda.

Christians should recognize with contrition that many churches are involved in the forms of economic injustice and racial discrimination which have created the conditions favourable to the growth of communism, and that the atheism and the anti-religious teaching of communism are in part a reaction to the chequered record of a professedly Christian society. It is one of the most fateful facts in modern history that often the working classes, including tenant farmers, came to believe that the churches were against them or indifferent to their plight. Christians should realize that the Church has often failed to offer to its youth the appeal that can evoke a disciplined, purposeful and sacrificial response, and that in this respect communism has for many filled a moral and psychological vacuum.

The points of conflict between Christianity and the atheistic Marxian communism of our day are as follows: (1) the communist promise of what amounts to a complete redemption of man in history; (2) the belief that a particular class by virtue of its role as the bearer of a new order is free from the sins and ambiguities that Christians believe to be characteristic of all human existence; (3) the materialistic and deterministic teachings, however they may be qualified, that are incompatible with belief in God and with the Christian view of man as a person, made in God's image and responsible to Him; (4) the ruthless methods of communists in dealing with their opponents; (5) the demand of the party on its members for an exclusive and unqualified loyalty which belongs only to God, and the coercive politics of communist dictatorship in controlling every aspect of life.

The Church should seek to resist the extension of any system, that not only includes oppressive elements but fails to provide any means by which the victims of oppression may criticize or act to correct it. It is a part of the mission of the Church to raise its voice of protest wherever men are the victims of terror, wherever they are denied such fundamental human rights as the right to be secure against arbitrary arrest, and wherever governments use torture and cruel punishments to intimidate the consciences of men.

The Church should make clear that there are conflicts between Christianity and capitalism. The developments of capitalism vary from country to country and often the exploitation of the workers that was characteristic of early capitalism has been corrected in considerable measure by the influence of trade unions, social legislation and responsible management. But (1) capitalism tends to subordinate what should be the primary task of any economy—the meeting of human needs— to the economic advantages of those who have most power over its institutions. (2) It tends to produce serious inequalities. (3) It has developed a practical form of materialism in western nations in spite of their Christian background, for it has placed the greatest emphasis upon success in making money. (4) It has also kept the people of capitalist countries subject to a kind of fate which has taken the form of such social catastrophes as mass unemployment.

The Christian churches should reject the ideologies of both communism and *laissez faire* capitalism, and should seek to draw men away from the false assumption that these extremes are the only alternatives. Each has made promises which it could not redeem. Communist ideology puts the emphasis upon economic justice, and promises that freedom will come automatically after the completion of the revolution. Capitalism puts the emphasis upon freedom, and promises that justice will follow as a by-product of free enterprise; that, too, is an ideology which has been proved false. It is the responsibility of Christians to seek new, creative solutions which never allow either justice or freedom to destroy the other.

V.   THE SOCIAL FUNCTION OF THE CHURCH

The greatest contribution that the Church can make to the renewal of society is for it to be renewed in its own life in faith and obedience to its Lord. Such inner renewal includes a clearer grasp of the meaning of the Gospel for the whole life of men. This renewal must take place both in the larger units of the Church and in the local congregations. The influence of worshipping congregations upon the problems of society is very great when those congregations include people from many social groups. If the Church can overcome the national and social barriers which now divide it, it can help society to overcome those barriers.

This is especially clear in the case of racial distinction. It is here that the Church has failed most lamentably, where it has reflected and then by its example sanctified the racial prejudice that is rampant in the world. And yet it is here that today its guidance concerning what God wills for it is especially clear. It knows that it must call society away from prejudice based upon race or colour and from the practices of discrimination and segregation as denials of justice and human dignity, but it cannot say a convincing word to society unless it takes steps to eliminate these practices from the Christian community because they contradict all that it believes about God's love for all His children.

There are occasions on which the churches, through their councils or through such persons as they may commission to speak on their behalf, should declare directly what they see to be the will of God for the public decisions of the hour. Such guidance will often take the form of warnings against concrete forms of injustice or oppression or social idolatry. They should also point to the main objectives toward which a particular society should move.

One problem is raised by the existence in several countries of Christian political parties. The Church as such should not be identified with any political party, and it must not act as though it were itself a political party. In general, the formation of such parties is hazardous because they easily confuse Christianity with the inherent compromises of politics. They may cut Christians off from the other parties which need the leaven of Christianity, and they may consolidate all who do not share the political principles of the Christian party not only against that party but against Christianity itself. Nevertheless, it may still be desirable in some situations for Christians to organize themselves into a political party for specific objectives, so long as they do not claim that it is the only possible expression of Christian loyalty in the situation.

But the social influence of the Church must come primarily from its influence upon its members through constant teaching and preaching of Christian truth in ways that illuminate the historical conditions in which men live and the problems which they face. The Church can be most effective in society as it inspires its members to ask in a new way what their Christian responsibility is whenever they vote or discharge the duties of public office, whenever they influence public opinion, whenever they make decisions as employers or as workers or in any other vocation to which they may be called. One of the most creative developments in the contemporary Church is the practice of groups of Christians facing much the same problems in their occupations to pray and take counsel together in order to find out what they should do as Christians.

In discussing the social function of the Church, Christians should always remember the great variety of situations in which the Church lives. Nations in which professing Christians are in the majority, nations in which the Church represents only a few per cent of the population, nations in which the Church lives under a hostile and oppressive Government offer very different problems for the Church. It is one of the contributions of the ecumenical experience of recent years that Churches under these contrasting conditions have come not only to appreciate one another's practices, but to learn from one another's failures and achievements and sufferings.

VI.   CONCLUSION

There is a great discrepancy between all that has been said here and the possibility of action in many parts of the world. Obedience to God will be possible under all external circumstances, and no one need despair when conditions restrict greatly the area of responsible action. The responsible society of which we have spoken represents, however, the goal for which the churches in all lands must work, to the glory of the one God and Father of all, and looking for the day of God and a new earth, wherein dwelleth righteousness.

Structures of Injustice and Struggles for Liberation
A Report from the Nairobi Assembly of the World Council of Churches, 1975

This was probably the most debated and controversial report adopted by the Fifth Assembly of the WCC. Addressed largely to Third World issues, it is more militant in tone and broader in scope than the Amsterdam Assembly's report on "the disorder of society" twenty-seven years before (see Appendix A). The report as a whole was adopted by a substantial majority of the delegates, and the human-rights amendment (paragraph 81, section 5) was accepted unanimously. Its many recommendations (paragraphs 74-90) were commended to the member churches for appropriate action. The text is from Breaking Barriers: Official Report of the World Council of Churches, Nairobi, 23 November–10 December, 1975, *edited by David M. Paton (London: SPCK, 1975), pages 100-119.*

Preamble

1. Structures of injustice and struggles of liberation pose a formidable challenge to the Church today. In striving to meet it, the Church has no other foundation on which to stand than it has in Jesus Christ. From him it has received its mandate: to witness to the truth which judges and to proclaim the good news which brings about freedom and salvation. In seeking its particular place in today's struggles for social justice and human liberation, the Church needs to be constantly guided by its divine mandate.

2. Whenever a Christian is confronted by structures of injustice and takes part in struggles for liberation, he or she is bound to experience the grip of destructive forces which are at work throughout the human family. Such forces give a taste of the "principalities and powers" of which Paul spoke.

3. The gospel brings us a message of God's total identification with humanity which is suffering under sin and other destructive powers. God's own solidarity with human beings is expressed in the reality of the servant Christ who humbled

himself to take up human form, who was born into poverty, who accepted the path of rejection, and who finally met his death on the cross. The vicarious suffering of Christ is the supreme manifestation of God's love. God in Christ took upon himself the whole burden of human sin and weakness.

4. God calls his Church, a community of forgiven sinners, to follow Christ on the same path committed to the cause of the poor, oppressed, and rejected, to declare the love of God by word and by the whole of life and to accept the cross.

5. The meaning of human suffering in itself is ambiguous. It both reflects the evils which plague the human race and it opens us to God's redeeming activity. In suffering for the cause of justice and for the sake of the gospel, the Church may participate in the vicarious suffering of Christ himself.

6. Is there readiness for suffering in our churches today? Or are our church structures built for our own protection and security and have they therefore become barriers which prevent us from sharing suffering in obedience to Christ and from receiving or reflecting God's redeeming love?

7. Christians who suffer together for the cause of justice and liberation find a deep experience of community with each other and with Christ. This community transcends differences of ideology, class, and Christian tradition. It is knit together by the power of forgiveness and love. It reflects the life of the ultimate community of the Triune God, and the expression of its deepest solidarity with the suffering and sinful humanity is the sharing of the Eucharist.

8. Suffering, however, is not the goal: beyond the cross is the resurrection. Christ has overcome the power of sin and death and broken the grip of the principalities and powers now still seemingly self-reinforcing and outside the control of persons involved. The victory of Christ therefore brings a tangible and deepened hope to those engaged in actual struggles against oppression and dominance. Moreover, his victory promises that the vicious circle in which injustice breeds more injustice and one form of oppression gives way to another form is being broken.

9. We realize that those who operate the structures of oppression are dependent on the people they oppress and that both are equally in need of liberation and God's forgiving love. In this fallen world, however, it is far more likely that the will and strength to end oppression come from those who bear the brunt of it in their own lives rather than from the privileged persons, groups, and nations.

10. Structures of injustice and struggles of liberation cannot be separated from each other. For practical purposes, however, we have divided this Report into three main sections: Human Rights, Sexism, and Racism.

HUMAN RIGHTS

Introduction

11. Our concerns for human rights are based on our conviction that God wills a society in which all can exercise full human rights. All human beings are created in God's image, to be equal, infinitely precious in God's sight and ours. Jesus Christ has bound us to one another by his life, death, and resurrection, so that what concerns one of us concerns us all.

12. Thus God's will and his love are intended for all and the struggle of Christians for human rights is a fundamental response to Jesus Christ. That gospel leads us to become ever more active in identifying and rectifying violations of human rights in our own societies, and to enter into new forms of ecumenical solidarity with Christians elsewhere who are similarly engaged. It leads us into the struggle of the poor and the oppressed both within and outside the Church as they seek to achieve their full human rights, and frees us to work together with people of other faiths or ideologies who share with us a common concern for human dignity.

13. In working for human rights we are often tempted to deal with symptoms rather than root causes. While we must work for the abolition of specific denials of human rights, such as torture, we must remember that unjust social structures, expressed through, e.g., economic exploitation, political manipulation, military power, class domination, psychological conditioning, create the conditions under which human rights are denied. To work for human rights, therefore, also means to work at the most basic level towards a society without unjust structures.

14. In our fallen world, there is no nation where human rights have been fully achieved. Because of discrepancies between what we profess and what we practise it is crucial for the churches to move from making *declarations* about human rights, to working for the full *implementation* of those rights. As Christians we affirm that the gospel brings about a human dignity which transcends our own human potential.

15. The world community has agreed upon certain high principles which are embodied in the Universal Declaration of Human Rights and the International Covenants on Human Rights. The recent Helsinki Declaration on Security and Co-operation in Europe gives, particularly for its signatories, a new potential for the implementation of these standards. These principles and standards largely coincide with our current Christian understanding about what makes up a just society.

16. Our chief task is to work for the realization of these enunciated rights *where we are*, but when there are those elsewhere who are powerless to cry out, we are called to be the voice of the voiceless and the advocates of the oppressed. In order to do this we must base our actions on accurate information. For this, open channels of communication are vitally important.

17. Common to all expressions of human rights is the right to self-determination by individuals, groups, and nations. The balance between these claims is always precarious, and their creative interrelationship may differ in various times and places. A distinction can be made, for example, between the limitation of rights due to all and the limitation of privileges available only to a few. Christians will need to assess different structures carefully, championing the rights of the individual when they are threatened by unjust structures and defending the rights of the majority when they are threatened by the tyranny of the few, and always bearing in mind that rights involve responsibilities.

18. Within this overall framework there are a number of specific human rights to which attention must be directed.

The Right to Basic Guarantees for Life

19. No rights are possible without the basic guarantees for life, including the right to work, to adequate food, to guaranteed health care, to decent housing, and to education for the full development of the human potential. Because women have the lowest status in most world communities their special needs should be recognized.

20. The ever-widening gap between rich and poor nations and between rich and poor within many nations has created today a highly explosive situation in which millions are denied these rights. This is due to a number of contributing factors, including the following:

(*a*) The present international economic structures are dominated by a few rich countries who control a large proportion of the world's resources and markets.

(*b*) Transnational corporations, often in league with oppressive regimes, distort and exploit the economies of poor nations.

(*c*) National economies are controlled in many cases by a small group of elites who also often give special access to transnational corporations.

(*d*) Patterns of land ownership are often exploitative.

21. The right to the basic guarantees for life involves guarding the rights of future generations, e.g., through protection of the environment and conservation of the earth's resources.

The Rights to Self-Determination and to Cultural Identity, and the Rights of Minorities

22. All people have the right freely to determine their political status and freely to pursue their economic, cultural, and social development. These rights are often violated by foreign governments and power systems, and through internal oppression and discrimination.

23. The churches should condemn such violations and take active part in efforts to ensure national sovereignty and self-determination for people who are deprived of them.

24. The churches must also defend and promote the rights of minorities (including that of migrant workers), be they cultural, linguistic, religious, ideological, or ethnic. Efforts to ensure that the Helsinki declaration be implemented could be of great importance in this context, especially for minorities in countries who have signed it.

25. The churches must closely scrutinize the reasoning of people in power when they seek to justify the violation of human rights for what they deem to be overriding concerns. Even in times of public emergency, fundamental rights such as the right to life and personal dignity, as defined by the Universal Declaration of Human Rights and the Covenants, should under no circumstances be derogated from.

The Right to Participate in Decision-Making within the Community

26. Participation of groups and individuals in the decision-making processes of the various communities in which they live is essential for achieving a truly dem-

ocratic society. As a precondition, there must be created an economic and social foundation which is in the interests of all segments of society. All members of the community, especially the young and women, should be educated in a spirit of social and political participation and responsibility. The structures of government on the national and local levels, within the religious communities, educational institutions, and in employment, must become more responsive to the will of all the persons belonging to these various communities, and must provide for protection against manipulation by powerful interests.

27. Women, because of their particular experience of oppression and the new insights they are receiving in the process of liberation, can often make a special contribution regarding participatory decision-making. They are exploring styles of shared leadership in which power and decision-making is horizontal rather than hierarchical, fluid rather than static. The Church, like the community, needs to receive this contribution, if it is to develop unifying and freeing structures.

28. Churches should participate in developing activity through which local communities of poor people, industrial and rural workers, women, minority groups, and others who suffer from any form of oppression can become aware of their condition and influence the course of the society.

The Right to Dissent

29. The right to dissent preserves a community or system from authoritarian rigidity. It is essential to the vitality of every society that the voices of dissenters be heard and that their right to hold opinions without interference, to freedom of expression, and to peaceful assembly be guaranteed. Christians, as followers of Jesus Christ, have a solidarity with the people who suffer because of their religious faith and practice and because of their stand in favour of political and social justice. Christian solidarity means a definite choice on the side of prisoners of conscience and political prisoners and refugees. The churches should make all efforts in their witness and intercessions, and by providing remedial assistance, to support those fellow human beings who suffer.

30. In readiness to reassess and to change their own structures and attitudes wherever necessary, the churches and the World Council of Churches itself must give all due attention within their communities to men, women, and young people who take a critical stand towards the predominant views and positions of their churches and of the World Council of Churches.

The Right to Personal Dignity

31. In many countries represented in this Section, evidence has been cited of gross violations of the right to personal dignity. Such violations include arbitrary arrest and imprisonment, torture, rape, deportation, child-battering, enforced hospitalization in mental hospitals, threats to families, and denial of habeas corpus. In some cases, prisoners and refugees are denied contact even with their families, thus becoming "non-persons." In other cases, arrested persons either disappear or are executed summarily.

32. The basic causes for these violations are to be found in the unjust social order, the abuse of power, the lack of economic development, and in unequal

development. This leads to violations of unjust laws and rebellion by the dispossessed, to which political and military forces of "law and order" respond with cruel repression. In some cases, the churches themselves have actively supported the oppressors or even become involved in the oppression itself, out of misguided convictions and/or attempts to safeguard their own privileges.

33. We also observe the increasing role, both nationally and internationally, of security police and para-police forces in the violation of the human right to personal dignity.

The Right to Religious Freedom

34. The right to religious freedom has been and continues to be a major concern of member churches and the WCC. However, this right should never be seen as belonging exclusively to the Church. The exercise of religious freedom has not always reflected the great diversity of convictions that exist in the world. This right is inseparable from other fundamental human rights. No religious community should plead for its own religious liberty without active respect and reverence for the faith and basic human rights of others.

35. Religious liberty should never be used to claim privileges. For the Church this right is essential so that it can fulfil its responsibilities which arise out of the Christian faith. Central to these responsibilities is the obligation to serve the whole community.

36. The right to religious freedom has been enshrined in most constitutions as a basic human right. By religious freedom we mean the freedom to have or to adopt a religion or belief of one's choice, and freedom, either individually or in community with others and in public or private, to manifest one's religion or belief in worship, observance, practice, and teaching. Religious freedom should also include the right and duty of religious bodies to criticize the ruling powers when necessary, on the basis of their religious convictions. In this context, it was noted that many Christians in different parts of the world are in prison for reasons of conscience or for political reasons as a result of their seeking to respond to the total demands of the gospel.

Human Rights and Christian Responsibility

37. Churches and other Christian communities carry, on the basis of the gospel, a special responsibility to express in word and deed their solidarity with those people whose human rights and fundamental freedoms are denied.

38. During its deliberations, the Section made frequent reference to the report of the consultation on "Human Rights and Christian Responsibility" held in St. Pölten, Austria, October 1974.

SEXISM

39. For the sake of the unity of the Church and humankind, the concerns of women must be consciously included in every aspect of the deliberations of the WCC. The liberation of women from structures of injustice must be taken seriously as seen in the light of the liberation of all oppressed people and all forms of discrimination.

40. At Amsterdam (1948) it was stated that "The Church, as the Body of Christ, consists of men and women, created as responsible persons to glorify God and to do God's will." Dr. W. A. Visser 't Hooft has added that "this truth, accepted in theory, is too often ignored in practice."

41. Despite efforts of the WCC in the past, the position of women, in both the Church and the world, has not changed significantly. As long as women are largely excluded from decision-making processes, they will be unable to realize a full partnership with men and therefore the Church will be unable to realize its full unity.

We wish to identify three areas in which change is necessary:

The Area of Theology:

42. A thorough examination needs to be made of the biblical and theological assumptions concerning the community of women and men in church and society.

43. Particular attention should be paid to the relationship of cultural assumptions and the way we understand the Word of God. Women and men in the Church are in need of clarification of the various biblical texts relating to the role of women in the story of creation and redemption.

These and other theological dimensions of our faith need to be re-examined, drawing heavily on the investigations of women as well as of theologians and scholars.

44. Language in many instances and the connotations of language in other instances fail to reflect the depth of the mystery of God who transcends all human metaphors and images. It is important that our language about God be inclusive (e.g., Isa. 49.15; 46.3-4; Matt. 23.37) to be true to the original biblical text. As the mother of Jesus, Mary embodies particular significance for Christian women and men. Her openness and willingness to respond to the call of God, in ways which were totally unexpected, proclaim to all people their responsibility to be free from any preconceived understandings as to how God works in and through people.

45. Also, it is important that the member churches of the WCC examine their liturgical language and practices with a view to eliminating sexist patterns so that women may join fully in the worshipping community.

The Area of Participation:

46. In order to be truly free, all people must participate in working towards their own liberation. This can be seen in all struggles for human rights and to overcome oppression.

47. The WCC must recognize the dimensions of powerlessness that affect women in the political, economic, social, and ecclesial areas of life. It should therefore continue its work, the work begun in International Women's Year, in working on the ten-year plan for action.

48. The model for this work should aim at providing funds for self-development and self-help programmes. We draw attention to the following vital areas:

(a) The urgent need to secure water supplies for women who are responsible for obtaining water for their community—in rural situations and others where water is not in easy supply;

(b) the need to facilitate indigenously-based self-help programmes which particularly relate to the needs of women, including the need to educate all women about the importance in all questions concerning their reproduction functions and the rights of their unborn children, and also regarding nutrition;

(c) the need to examine the relationship women hold to the law—both judicial and customary law (e.g. dowry systems), family law, inheritance law, contract and loan law. Women also need to be helped to understand their rights under present legal systems;

(d) the need to recognize that where racism is involved women are the most disadvantaged group of all.

The Area of Relationship:

49. A third area of urgent concern is the interrelationship of women and men who frequently exploit one another. This exploitation often takes the form of misuse of power over each other which is linked with lack of understanding of their mutual identity.

50. People need to feel independent, valuable, and secure in the totality of their identity as men and women before they can relate to each other in mutual interdependence.

51. For this to happen it is essential that women unite in supportive groups to find solidarity with their sisters, and a new sense of worth. Such a discovery of worth is essential for the full development of equal partnership.

52. We recognize that men and women together form one corporate body in Christ and that they cannot be seen in separation from each other; nevertheless, evidence shows that in many marriage relationships women and men are unable to develop their full personhood. The Christian Church is in a key position to foster and support the partners to marriage in their search for mutuality.

53. The Church is in the same unique position in respect to persons living in different life situations (e.g. single people living in isolation, single parents), extended families, and persons living in communal patterns. There is evidence that these people are not fully accepted by many societies and are often ignored by the Church.

54. In the social relationships between women and men, the dynamics that are set up by oppression are such that women have a particular understanding of, and interest in, reconciliation of confrontation and conflict. They are emphatic that those who are liberated from oppression should not become the oppressor in the same structures. This can only prevent true liberation and perpetuate conflict.

55. Recognizing that small advances in the position of women in church and society have been made, we are nevertheless convinced that it is vital for the WCC and the member churches to open all service opportunities to women and to encourage the study, by both men and women, of a deeper and more thorough participation of women in church life with special attention to the question of ordination and the employment of women in the Church.

56. The freedom and unity of Jesus Christ includes both halves of the human community; therefore it is imperative to the unity of church and society that the full participation of women be given urgent consideration and immediate implementation.

RACISM

Fundamental Convictions

57. Racism is a sin against God and against fellow human beings. It is contrary to the justice and the love of God revealed in Jesus Christ. It destroys the human dignity of both the racist and the victim. When practised by Christians it denies the very faith we profess and undoes the credibility of the Church and its witness to Jesus Christ. Therefore, we condemn racism in all its forms both inside and outside the Church.

58. When we again try to deal with racism at this Assembly we cannot but begin by confessing our conscious and unconscious complicity in racism and our failures to eradicate it even from our own house. In previous Assemblies we have many times affirmed as churches our common rejection of racism. Yet, we still find ourselves only at the beginning. We stand in need of God's forgiveness and grace which will free us from our complicity and failures, towards a new commitment, to strive for the justice that will bring an end to all racism.

59. The past years of struggle against racism have shown that we as churches need a more profound understanding of the nature and of all varied manifestations of racism. We need to confront it with the fullness of the biblical message, to see more deeply its demonic character, and also to comprehend its psychological, economic, and social impact on persons and communities and its roots in societies. However, although our understanding needs to grow, we already know more than enough to participate in obedience to Christ in the fight against the manifestations of racism in politics and in the Church.

60. Concerning the methods to be used in the fight against racism, we join the agonizing search for guidelines on how to deal with the inevitable question of violence and non-violence. A helpful contribution to this search has been made in the paper "Violence, Non-violence, and the Struggle for Social Justice" (commended by the WCC Central Committee, 1973).

The Scope of Racism—a Litany of Shame

61. Racism can be seen today in every part of the world. No nation is totally free of it. Its victims cross the paths of most of us daily. Yet, it is obvious that some of our countries are more visibly plagued by it than others, e.g., where racism is legally enforced. We heard in the Section from every continent a series of passionate pleas to draw the common attention of the churches here to the outrageous expressions of racism in their respective countries, like a litany of shame of the whole human family. However, it brought home the growing urgency of the problem of racism on every continent.

62. There is much evidence that racially oppressed communities are rapidly becoming aware of the injustices to which they are subjected and that they more and more refuse to endure indignity and exploitation. Consequently, they are increasingly determined to liberate themselves and thereby affirm their humanity. We need to express our solidarity with them.

63. It also became obvious that racism is a factor in numerous violations of human rights and fundamental freedoms as dealt with in another part of this Report.

Racism in Churches

64. To our shame, Christian churches around the world are all too often infected by racism, overt and covert. Examples of it include the following:

(a) churches and congregations have been and are still being organized along racially exclusive lines;

(b) congregations welcome to their fellowship warmly those who are like the majority of its members, but easily reject those who are different;

(c) many argue that they are free of racism as if its reality could be undone by ignoring it;

(d) churches frequently contribute to the psychological conditioning of the racially oppressed so that they will not sense the racism imposed upon them;

(e) they are more willing to support struggles against racism far from home than to face the racism which is practised on their doorstep;

(f) churches often reflect the racially prejudiced attitudes of their governments, their elites, and self-pretensions, while presuming that their own attitudes arise out of Christian faith;

(g) in leadership privileges and in programmatic priorities churches tend too easily to indulge in racism without even recognizing it.

65. We recognize that the Spirit of God does break through structural and other barriers so that Christian communities do from time to time rise to challenge their own racism and to seek models of commitment to a non-racist Christian faith, even if for every such sign of hope there remain too many examples of denial.

Institutional Racism

66. Pervasive as individual attitudes and acts of racism may be, the major oppressive racism of our time is imbedded in institutional structures that reinforce and perpetuate themselves, generally to the great advantage of the few and the disadvantage of many. Examples of this:

(a) racism openly enforced by law;

(b) predominantly white North Atlantic nations create trade patterns and preferences that militate against other racial groups;

(c) strong military powers and other industrialized countries supply sophisticated arms and assistance to racist regimes;

(d) powerful countries, without regard to their social system, often entrench themselves in supporting racial repression under the pretence of legally justified defence of their own national self-interest;

(e) continued patterns of settler colonialism contribute to racial oppression;

(f) the powerful in affluence, education, ecclesiastical position, or secular authority, tend to protect their systems of privilege and to shut out of the decision-making any influence of the weak and the subordinate. Moreover, they tend to overlay their racism privileges all too often with an aura of kindliness and service.

67. Institutionalized racism, in its many structural forms, resists most challenges with careful concessions calculated to preserve its power. We reject a conspiratorial theory of history that oversimplifies the complex struggles of humanity for liberation by describing all institutions with power as pernicious and all powerless peoples as virtuous. This does not, however, make us blind to the evident inclination of current power structures to perpetuate racism. All these institutional forms of racism need to be carefully analysed and as Christians we need to attack them with prophetic word and action.

Interdependence of Oppression

68. We lift up for special attention the fact that across the globe racist structures reinforce each other internationally. Self-serving policies of transnational corporations operate across boundaries with impunity; weapons or mercenaries are supplied internationally to local elites; the worldwide communications networks are manipulated to reinforce racist attitudes and actions. It is precisely because of this world-wide web of racist penetration that the churches must seek out policies and programmes at ecumenical and international levels. Such programmes can expose international systems which support racism and provide an effective counter-response to them.

69 In this connection it should be noted that churches and their foreign mission agencies in the West ought to re-examine their use of human and material resources so that they can effectively support liberation efforts and contribute to human dignity in developing countries in ways that are beyond the scope of traditional patterns of giving and receiving.

70. The multinational character of racist structures also makes necessary a constant vigilance by Christians so that they are ready to speak and act and that the pressure of international challenges to racism is felt and felt strongly, and the victims of racism may know that they are not abandoned and that their liberation is essential to the liberation of all.

The Urgency of the Task of the Churches

71. The grip of racism is today as acute as ever because of its institutional penetration, its reinforcement by military and economic power and because of widespread fear of loss of privilege by the affluent world.

72. This gives a special urgency to the task of the churches both in facing and eradicating racism within themselves and their home countries and in strengthening their international efforts against racism.

73. Southern Africa deserves continued priority in the churches' combined efforts because of the churches' own involvement in the area and because of the legal enforcement of racism there. African delegates brought forcefully before us the need of churches to practise what they preach. What is at stake is the faithfulness to the fullness of the message entrusted to the Church.

RECOMMENDATIONS

ON SEXISM

74. Whereas a thorough examination needs to be made of the biblical and theological assumptions concerning the community of women and men in the Church, *it is recommended that* the WCC shall commend the study document "The Community of Women and Men in the Church" (1975) to its member churches and invite their active participation in a three-year study in which:

1. priority be given to a theological study of sexuality, taking into account the culture of the member churches;

2. women theologians and scholars be invited to participate fully in the study;

3. care be taken in translations of the word of God, which always comes in human language, so that they reflect the gender used in the original language, and to consider developing principles for the elimination of sexist terminology, if any, in our languages.

75. Whereas there is ample evidence that the expertise and gifts of women are not being fully used by any Church, *it is recommended that* the WCC shall urge:

1. member churches to consider making available funds for theological education of women (especially advanced study);

2. member churches to ensure full participation of women in all decision-making bodies;

3. those churches that ordain women to give them the same opportunities and pay as men, according to the measure of their gifts (1 Cor. 12);

4. those member churches which have agreed in principle to the ordination of women to the priesthood/ministry to take immediate action to admit women to all their ordained ministries, taking into serious consideration that there are other churches of our WCC fellowship that are not in agreement with this practice;

5. those member churches which do ordain women and those which do not continue dialogue with each other and with non-member churches about the full participation of women in the full life of the Church including ordained ministries, according to the measure of their gifts.

76. Whereas men and women in some parts of the world are living at subsistence level, while others are living at adequate and more than adequate levels; and whereas women have special responsibilities for bringing new life into the world, nurturing and rearing children, *it is recommended that* the WCC shall urge its member churches and those present at this Assembly to encourage women and men to:

1. realize that all those who benefit from the economic exploitation of other people in any part of the world have to share the responsibility for such exploitation, even if they are not directly involved; and to act to bring pressure on governments, transnational corporations, and other bodies whenever they are oppressive;

2. participate fully in the ecclesial, political, economic, and social structures of their own societies at all levels to change these towards a more just society;

3. help local congregations and communities to study and implement the UN

Ten Point World Plan of Action (cf. 47);

    4. support women by facilitating and funding specific projects such as:

        (a) securing safe water supplies (cf. 48 a);

        (b) fostering indigenously-based self-help programmes (cf. 48 b);

        (c) educating women about their legal rights (cf. 48 c);

        (d) establishing programmes in congregations to study and implement the proposals of the WCC's Consultation on Sexism in the '70s as found in the report, "Discrimination Against Women," published in 1975;

        (e) supporting those organizations which are working to eliminate discrimination against women in political, economic, social, and ecclesial areas of life (cf. 47).

77. Whereas we recognize the urgent need to examine ways in which women and men can grow into a partnership of mutual interdependence, *it is recommended that* the WCC urge its member churches to:

    1. affirm the personhood and mutual interdependence of individuals in families;

    2. affirm the personhood and worth of people living in different life situations (cf. 53);

    3. act upon these affirmations so as to enable women to realize their potential in every area of life;

    4. actively support programmes which investigate the exploitation of human sexuality for gain and seek to assist individuals who are exploited.

78. Whereas these recommendations have such important implications for the Church, *it is further recommended that:*

all member churches, especially their women's organizations, shall be urged to support women's concerns through special funds earmarked for the Women's Desk and to ask the WCC to appoint an additional staff member to co-ordinate the work.

ON HUMAN RIGHTS

Education and Conscientization on Human Rights

79. The churches should:

    1. seek to raise Christian and public awareness of violations of human rights and their causes, developing educational materials for this purpose;

    2. educate their constituencies, particularly at congregational levels, to their rights and the legal recourses available to them;

    3. develop further technical expertise on human rights, perhaps through the creation of human rights institutes related to national and regional ecumenical bodies and providing scholarships for the study of human rights;

    4. in the light of the increasing incidence of torture and inhuman treatment of prisoners in many parts of the world, promote instruction on human rights and moral responsibility in the training of police and military personnel;

    5. include human rights in the formation of pastors, priests, and lay leaders, and in the curricula of other church training centres, such as development education institutions.

Information and Contacts

80. The churches should:

1. gather and disseminate information on different approaches to human rights, and on the basis of human rights;

2. gather reliable information on human rights violations in their own societies and elsewhere;

3. analyze such violations in order to discover their causes, reminding their constituencies regularly of how specific injustices reflect unjust social structures and seeking to avoid complicity with them;

4. develop effective channels of communication with one another, through personal contacts or otherwise, in order to ensure reliability of information and real effectiveness of active expressions of solidarity;

5. recognize, as a priority, that in the Middle East the rights of the Palestinian people under occupation should be implemented and work towards that end;

6. where the rights of entire peoples are violated through colonial domination; undue political, economic, or military interference in their national affairs; occupation of their lands by foreign powers; expulsion from their homelands; self-imposed racist, military, or other oppressive regimes—look beyond the propaganda of the offending power to the realities of those who suffer and help Christians and others to understand the true nature of their plight and struggles for their just rights. In co-operation with regional ecumenical bodies, the WCC should assist the churches in this task.

Legal Machinery for the Protection of Human Rights

81. The churches should:

1. help create new, improve existing, and facilitate access to legal institutions for the defence and promotion of human rights at community, national, and international levels;

2. seek access to prisons, camps, and other places of detention in order to obtain complete and accurate information about the treatment of inmates and conditions of detention, and defend the prisoners' rights to regular contact with family, friends, and legal counsel.

Action at Local, National, and Regional Levels

3. The struggle of the people themselves for their own rights is fundamentally important. Local congregations should become more active in identifying, documenting, and combating violations of human rights in their own communities. They and their national churches should seek ways to support the struggles of peoples, groups, and individuals for their own legitimate rights, helping them to form networks of solidarity to strengthen one another in their struggles.

4. Particular attention should be given to the special needs of political prisoners and refugees. In some cases, pastoral care becomes an act of courage, yet Christ calls us to minister both materially and spiritually to those in prison and to the outcasts as well as to their families.

5. Many changes are taking place in Asian governments. There is martial law in Taiwan; crisis government in the Philippines; emergency rule in India and South Korea; military rule in Bangladesh; one-party states in such countries as the People's Republic of China. In all other countries of Asia (e.g. Malaysia, Singapore, Australia, New Zealand, Indonesia, Japan) there are also violations of human rights. Wherever human rights are suppressed or violated by any Asian government, churches have a duty to work for the defence of human rights, especially of the oppressed. We believe the whole question of the mission of the Church is involved in this issue and urge churches to work for the rights of the people of Asia to participate in their own development.

6. Regional ecumenical bodies should help their churches to become more active in responding to the human rights needs of their societies. Work like that of the Christian Conference of Asia, and the consultation on "Human Rights and the Churches in Africa," sponsored by the All Africa Conference of Churches in collaboration with CCIA should be encouraged and pursued, and work like that of the interpretation programme of the MECC.

7. The report of the consultation on "Human Rights and Christian Responsibility" is commended to the churches for appropriate study and action (St Pölten, Austria, October 1974).

Responsibility of the WCC

82. The WCC should:

1. aid the churches in the above tasks;

2. gather and disseminate information about human rights violations within the limits of its possibilities;

3. help strengthen church leaders and Christians to perform the difficult tasks which face them, and to execute conscientiously their prophetic role in the face of abuses of power and inhuman practices in their churches, communities, and national societies;

4. provide a place for mutual challenge of the churches to become better servants; a place where the churches come together to give one another pastoral and material support as they become more courageously engaged in the struggle for human rights where they are; and a place to share strategies for struggle;

5. when necessary and appropriate, send pastoral and/or information-gathering teams to places where Christians and others are in need of support and encouragement in their own struggles for human rights;

6. use its consultative relationship with the UN, its possibilities to approach regional inter-governmental bodies and individual governments, and its co-operation with other non-governmental organizations in efforts to bring an end to human rights violations;

7. directly or through the CCIA issue public statements on violations of nations', groups', or individuals' human rights where this could serve those directly affected and, through clarifying the issues involved, contribute to the elimination of the root causes of such violations;

8. aid, materially and otherwise, groups and individuals who, because of their efforts to act out their Christian faith in defending human rights and in struggling

for justice in their societies, have become the objects of harassment, repression, imprisonment, or persecution.

ON RACISM

83. We commend the Programme to Combat Racism to the member churches, and urge them to ensure that their members receive accurate information about the whole programme. We ask for further support of the Programme in terms of increased commitment, prayer, and finance, in order that the various aspects of the Programme, e.g. theological reflection, action-oriented research, information, Annual Project List and Special Fund, may be even more effective.

84. Of primary importance to the churches' involvement in the struggle against racism is theological reflection on racism and on methods of combating it. We therefore draw to the churches' attention the ongoing joint project of the Programme to Combat Racism and Faith and Order and its report on a recent consultation, "Racism in Theology and Theology against Racism" (WCC 1975). We also encourage the study and implementation of the report on "Violence, Non-violence, and the Struggle for Social Justice," commended to the member churches by the Central Committee (Geneva 1973).

85. We urge member churches to ensure, wherever possible, the active participation of representatives from minority and racially oppressed groups in decision-making concerning their welfare and well-being within the life of churches and of society.

86. We urge member churches to provide factual information, gained from the oppressed groups themselves, so that Christians can learn the extent of their involvement in structures that perpetuate racial injustice and have recourse to specific proposals for responsible ecumenical action.

87. South Africa, which highlights racism in its most blatant form, must retain high priority for the attention of the member churches. Apartheid is possible only with the support of a large number of Christians there. We urge member churches to identify with, and wherever possible initiate or activate, campaigns to halt arms traffic; to work for the withdrawal of investments and the ending of bank loans; to stop white migration. These issues have already been urged by the WCC and we recommend these for urgent action by the member churches. Their implementation would be an effective non-violent contribution to the struggle against racism.

88. Racism, as a world problem, however, also demands the churches' attention in other particular situations, including

(a) the plight of the Korean minority in Japan;

(b) the condition of the native peoples of North and South America;

(c) the situation of the aboriginal peoples of Australia and ethnic minorities in New Zealand;

(d) growing racism against black people and migrant workers in Europe.

89. Churches everywhere should beware that their commendable zeal for combating racism and other forms of ethnocentrism in distant lands should not lead to ignoring its manifestations in their midst.

90. In all this, churches should be making a conscious effort to be themselves models of non-racist communities.

APPENDIX C

Organization of the World Council of Churches

In 1976 the World Council, whose headquarters staff (the General Secretariat) is in Geneva, Switzerland, was reorganized into three major program units incorporating fifteen functions and concerns. The Faith and Order emphasis and the Church and Society emphasis were placed in the Faith and Witness unit, and the Program to Combat Racism was placed in the Justice and Service unit. The chart below shows the organization of the Council in simplified form.

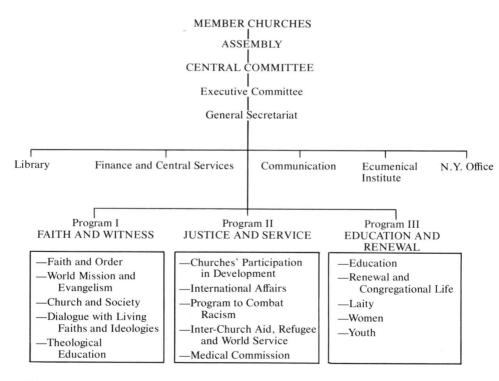

MEMBER CHURCHES

ASSEMBLY

CENTRAL COMMITTEE

Executive Committee

General Secretariat

Library   Finance and Central Services   Communication   Ecumenical Institute   N.Y. Office

Program I FAITH AND WITNESS	Program II JUSTICE AND SERVICE	Program III EDUCATION AND RENEWAL
—Faith and Order —World Mission and Evangelism —Church and Society —Dialogue with Living Faiths and Ideologies —Theological Education	—Churches' Participation in Development —International Affairs —Program to Combat Racism —Inter-Church Aid, Refugee and World Service —Medical Commission	—Education —Renewal and Congregational Life —Laity —Women —Youth

Major Ecumenical Meetings

The World Council of Churches, established in 1948, emerged from a series of ecumenical meetings that began with the World Missionary Conference in 1910. The list below includes major conferences before and after 1948 and indicates the two chief concerns of the movement— Faith and Order, and Life and Work (later called Church and Society).

PRE–WORLD COUNCIL OF CHURCHES

World Missionary Conference
1910, Edinburgh

Faith and Order
1927, Lausanne
1937, Edinburgh

Life and Work
1925, Stockholm
1937, Oxford

Committee of Fourteen
1938, Utrecht

WORLD COUNCIL OF CHURCHES

First Assembly
1948, Amsterdam

Second Assembly
1954, Evanston

Third Assembly
1961, New Delhi

Major Conferences
Church and Society
1966, Geneva

Fourth Assembly
1968, Uppsala

Salvation Today
1973, Bangkok

Fifth Assembly
1975, Nairobi

Faith, Science, Future
1979, Boston

The Special Fund to Combat Racism

A Statement by the World Council of Churches, 1973

After an introductory paragraph, this September 1973 statement repeats the criteria for the Special Fund to Combat Racism established by the Executive Committee in 1970 and reconfirmed in 1971. It is from a WCC press release.

As the struggle of the racially oppressed for justice and liberation intensifies, so their needs increase. Through the Special Fund, the World Council of Churches has taken a lead in terms of moral and financial support for their humanitarian programs. The grants have started an educational process in the member churches without precedent. Christians all over the world are forced to review their relationships to oppressor and oppressed. This process must be continued, and the grants will play an important role, provoking Christians to take more seriously the faith they profess and to discern more clearly its implications for their role in society.

In September 1970, the World Council of Churches Executive Committee adopted the following criteria for the Special Fund:

1. The purpose of the organizations must not be inconsonant with the general purposes of the World Council of Churches and its Units, and the grants are to be made and used for humanitarian activities (social, health and education purposes, legal aid, etc.).

2. The proceeds of the Fund shall be used to support organizations that combat racism, rather than welfare organizations which alleviate the effects of racism, which would normally be eligible for support from other units of the World Council of Churches.

3. The focus of the grants should be on raising the level of awareness and on strengthening the organizational capabilities of oppressed people. In addition, there is a need to support organizations that align themselves with the victims of racial injustice and pursue the same objectives.

4. The grants are made without control over the manner in which they are spent, but are intended as an expression of commitment by the Program to Combat

Racism to the cause of economic, social and political justice which these organizations promote.

5. The situation in Southern Africa is recognized as priority due to the overt and intensive nature of white racism and the increasing awareness on the part of oppressed people in their struggle for liberation. In the selection of other areas, we have taken account of those areas where the struggle is most intensive and where a grant might make a substantial contribution to the process of liberation, particularly where racial groups are in imminent danger of being physically or culturally exterminated.

6. Grants should be made with due regard to where they can have maximum effect. Token grants should not be made unless there is a possibility of their eliciting substantial response from other organizations.

These criteria were re-confirmed by the Executive Committee at its meeting in September 1971.

Program to Combat Racism: Grants, 1970-1978

In its first nine years the WCC's Program to Combat Racism gave $3,063,545 to more than a hundred organizations in nearly thirty countries. Almost 65 per cent went to groups attempting to overthrow white regimes (and in 1978, two interracial regimes) in southern Africa and to other organizations supporting radical political change in that region. The table on the following pages shows the grants, by country, in current U.S. dollars. (None were made in 1972.) The form of the table and the figures for 1970-76 (with a few revisions from WCC-supplied data) are from Darril Hudson, The World Council of Churches in International Affairs *(Leighton Buzzard, Great Britain: The Faith Press, 1977); the 1977 figures are from an Ecumenical Press Service release; and the 1978 figures are from the Institute for the Study of Conflict, London.*

	1970	1971	1973	1974	1975	1976	1977	1978
AFRICA								
Angola								
National Union for the Total Independence of Angola (União Nacional Para a Independencia Total de Angola, UNITA)...........	10,000	7,500	6,000	14,000	—	—	—	—
People's Movement for the Liberation of Angola (Movimento Popular de Libertação de Angola, MPLA).........	20,000	25,000	10,000	23,000	—	—	—	—
Revolutionary Government of Angola in Exile (Governo Revolucionario de Angola no Exil, GRAE)	20,000	7,500	10,000	23,000	—	—	—	—
Guinea-Bissau								
African Independence Party of Guinea and Cape Verde Islands (Partido Africano da Independencia da Guiné e Cabo Verde, PAIGC)	20,000	25,000	25,000	100,000	—	—	—	—
Mozambique								
Mozambique Institute of FRELIMO (Frente de Libertação de Moçambique)	15,000	20,000	25,000	60,000	—	—	—	—
Rhodesia								
African National Council (Zimbabwe)	—	—	—	—	83,500	28,355	—	—
Zimbabwe African National Union (ZANU)	10,000	5,000	—	15,000	—	28,355	—	—
Zimbabwe African People's Union (ZAPU)	10,000	5,000	—	15,000	—	28,335	—	—
Zimbabwe Liberation Struggle (Patriotic Front)	—	—	—	—	—	—	85,000*	(85,000*)
South Africa								
African National Congress (South Africa)	—	—	2,500	15,000	45,000	50,000	25,000	25,000
Lutuli Memorial Foundation of African National Congress	10,000	5,000	—	15,000	—	—	—	—
Pan Africanist Congress of Azania	—	—	2,500	15,000	45,000	50,000	25,000	25,000
South African Congress of Trade Unions	—	—	—	—	—	5,000	5,000	5,000
South West Africa (Namibia)								
South West African People's Organization (SWAPO)	5,000	25,000	20,000	30,000	83,500	85,000	125,000	125,000
Tanzania								
Sixth Pan African Congress	—	—	—	12,000	—	—	—	—
Zambia								
Africa 2000 Project	15,000	5,000	—	—	—	—	—	—
Total Africa	135,000	130,000	101,000	322,000	257,045	275,000	265,000	180,000

*Authorized in 1977 but awarded in 1978.

	1970	1971	1973	1974	1975	1976	1977	1978
ASIA AND AUSTRALASIA								
Australia								
Aboriginal and Islanders Development Fund	—	—	—	—	10,000	—	—	—
Aboriginal Community Organization Course	—	—	—	—	—	—	—	12,000
Campaign Against Racial Exploitation	—	—	—	—	—	—	—	5,000
Federal Council for the Advancement of Aborigines and Torres Strait Islanders	10,000	—	14,000	—	—	10,000	—	—
Kimberley Aboriginal Land Council	—	—	—	—	—	—	12,500	12,500
National Tribal Council	15,000	—	—	—	—	—	—	—
North Queensland Land Rights Committee	—	—	—	—	—	—	7,500	17,500
Southern Africa Liberation Centre	—	—	—	—	—	5,000	5,000	5,000
Japan								
Anti-Apartheid Movement of Osaka, Japan	2,000	—	—	—	—	5,000	—	—
International Committee to Combat the Immigration Bill in Japan	—	—	—	—	—	—	—	—
Japan Anti-Apartheid Committee, Youth Section	—	5,000	—	—	7,500	—	5,000	5,000
Legal Defence Committee in Japan (Korean Minority)	—	—	—	10,000	—	—	—	—
National Committee Combating Discrimination against Ethnic People	—	—	—	—	20,000	—	10,000	—
New Hebrides								
New Hebrides National Party	—	—	—	—	—	10,000	10,000	—
New Zealand								
National Anti-Apartheid Co-ordinating Committee	—	—	—	4,000	—	7,500	—	5,000
Total Asia and Australasia	27,000	5,000	14,000	14,000	37,500	37,500	50,000	62,000
SOUTH AMERICA AND THE CARIBBEAN								
XLII Congreso Internacional de Americanistas	—	—	—	—	—	13,000	—	—
Bolivia								
Bolivian Project in Aid of Indian Liberation (Proyecto de Acción Liberadora de Indígena en Bolivia)	—	12,500	—	—	—	—	—	—
Centro de Coordinación y Promoción Campesina	—	—	—	—	20,000	—	—	—
Colombia								
Asociación Nacional de Usuarios Campesinos	—	—	—	—	15,000	10,000	—	—
Colombian Foundation for the Defence of Natural Resources and Black Workers (Fundación Colombiana para la Defensa de los Recursos Naturales y de los Trabajadores Negros)	—	—	10,000	—	—	—	—	—

	1970	1971	1973	1974	1975	1976	1977	1978
Committee for the Defence of the Indian in Colombia (Coordinación de Movimientos Indígenas en Colombia)	15,000	5,000	—	—	—	—	—	—
Indigenous Rural Alliance in Struggle for the Land (Alianza Campesina Indígena en Lucha por la Tierra)	—	—	—	15,000	—	—	—	—
Native Regional Council of the Cauca (Consejo Regional Indígena del Cauca, CRIC)	—	—	10,000	10,000	5,000	15,000	15,000	15,000
Ecuador								
Imbabura Indian Peasant Organization	—	—	—	—	20,000	—	—	—
Mexico								
Centro Antropologico de Documentación de America Latine (CADAL)	—	—	—	—	—	—	7,500	—
Paraguay								
Indigenist Association of Paraguay (Asociación Indigenista del Paraguay)	—	2,500	—	—	—	—	—	—
Caribbean								
Christian Action for Development in the Eastern Caribbean	—	5,000	—	—	—	—	—	—
Total South America and Caribbean	15,000	25,000	20,000	25,000	60,000	38,000	22,500	15,000

NORTH AMERICA

Canada

	1970	1971	1973	1974	1975	1976	1977	1978
Committee for Original Peoples Entitlement (COPE)	—	—	—	—	—	10,000	—	—
Hunters and Trappers Organization	—	—	—	—	—	—	—	12,500
Indian Brotherhood of the Northwest Territories (DENE)	—	—	—	—	—	—	15,000	17,500
Indian Brotherhood of the Northwest Territories (IB.NWT)	—	—	7,500	—	—	—	—	—
Inuit (Eskimo) Tapirisat of Canada	—	2,500	—	—	—	—	—	—
National Indian Brotherhood (on behalf of Cree—Inuit Council of James Bay)	—	—	7,500	5,000	6,000	6,000	5,000	—
Toronto Committee for the Liberation of Southern Africa	—	—	—	—	—	—	—	5,000

United States of America

	1970	1971	1973	1974	1975	1976	1977	1978
Akwesasne Notes	—	—	—	—	5,000	—	5,000	—
Au African News Service (AANS); for 1975 and 1977, see Southern Africa Committee, below	—	—	3,000	—	—	5,000	—	—
American Indian Movement (AIM)	—	—	6,000	15,000	15,000	15,000	—	—
Americans for Indian Opportunity (Oklahoma Indians)	—	—	—	5,000	—	—	—	—
Center for National Security Studies: Africa Project	—	—	—	—	7,500	—	—	—

	1970	1971	1973	1974	1975	1976	1977	1978
Coalition of Concerned Black Americans (earlier, Legal Protection of Civil Rights of Minorities in the USA)	—	7,500	6,000	—	—	—	—	—
Delta Ministry, Mississippi	—	—	—	—	15,000	15,000	10,000	—
El Paso Education Research Project	—	—	5,000	—	—	—	—	—
Free Southern Theatre	—	—	—	5,000	5,000	—	—	—
Haitian Refugee Concerns	—	—	—	—	—	10,000	10,000	—
Indian Law Resource Center	—	—	—	—	—	—	—	12,500
Indigena	—	—	—	—	—	—	5,000	—
Institute for the Development of Indian Law in Washington, D.C.	—	2,500	—	—	—	—	—	—
Institute of the Black World	—	—	—	—	—	—	10,000	—
International Indian Treaty Council	—	—	—	—	—	—	10,000	12,500
Malcolm X Liberation University	—	7,500	6,000	—	—	—	—	—
National Association for the Advancement of Colored People—Legal Defense Fund	—	—	—	—	—	10,000	—	—
National Conference of Black Lawyers	—	—	—	—	—	—	—	12,500
National Indian Youth Council	—	—	—	—	—	—	15,000	12,500
Puerto Rico Solidarity Committee	—	—	—	—	—	15,000	5,000	5,000
Southern Africa Committee (in 1975 and 1977, grant shared with AANS)	—	—	—	4,000	5,000	—	5,000	—
Southern Election Fund Inc.	—	7,500	—	—	—	—	—	—
United Farm Workers Organizing Committee AFL-CIO	—	2,500	—	15,000	15,000	15,000	—	—
Washington Office on Africa	—	—	—	—	—	5,000	—	—
Total North America	—	30,000	41,000	49,000	73,500	106,000	95,000	90,000

EUROPE

Belgium

	1970	1971	1973	1974	1975	1976	1977	1978
Belgian Anti-Apartheid Committee (Comité de Soutien à la Lutte Contre le Colonialisme et l'Apartheid) (1976 total shared with Aktiekomitee Zuidelijk Afrika and Boycot Outspan Aktie)	—	2,500	2,000	—	6,000	7,500	—	7,500

France

	1970	1971	1973	1974	1975	1976	1977	1978
Association des Marocains en France	—	—	—	—	—	—	—	—
Campaign Campagne Anti-Outspan	—	—	—	—	5,000	—	10,000	5,000
Collectif des Organisations Africaines en France	—	—	—	—	5,000	10,000	10,000	20,000
Comité des Travailleurs Algériens en France	—	—	—	—	5,000	10,000	10,000	—
French Anti-Apartheid Committee (Comité Français Contre l'Apartheid)	—	2,500	—	—	—	—	—	—

	1970	1971	1973	1974	1975	1976	1977	1978
Germany								
Informationsstelle Südliches Afrika and Anti-Apartheid Bewegung	—	—	—	—	6,000	6,000	5,000	7,500
Italy								
Liberazione e Sviluppo	—	—	—	—	—	5,000	—	—
Netherlands								
Angola Committee and Dr Eduardo Mondlane Foundation, for their Foundation for Information about Racism and Colonialism (in 1975, grant shared with Anti-Apartheid Movement and Boycot Outspan Aktie)	5,000	—	2,000	4,000	10,000	—	—	—
Anti-Apartheid Movement	—	—	—	4,000	—	—	—	—
Boycot Outspan Aktie	—	—	—	—	—	5,000	—	—
Switzerland								
Anti-Apartheid Movement	—	—	2,000	4,000	5,000	5,000	5,000	—
United Kingdom								
The Africa Bureau	2,500	—	—	—	—	—	—	—
The Anti-Apartheid Movement	5,000	—	2,000	4,000	10,000	10,000	—	5,000
Committee for Freedom in Mozambique, Angola and Guinea	—	—	—	4,000	—	—	—	—
Europe-Africa Research Project—Black Press International, later Europe-Third World Research Centre	—	—	—	5,000	—	—	—	—
'Free University for Black Studies'	—	2,500	—	—	—	—	—	—
The Hong Kong Research Project	—	2,500	—	—	—	—	—	—
Institute of Race Relations, UK	—	—	—	—	—	—	7,500	—
International Defence and Aid Fund	—	—	7,500	—	5,000	5,000	5,000	12,500
Joint Council for the Welfare of Immigrants	3,000	—	—	—	—	—	—	—
Namibia Support Committee	—	—	—	—	—	—	10,000	12,500
Race Today Collective Association	—	—	—	—	—	—	—	5,000
West Indian Standing Conference	7,500	—	—	10,000	15,000	30,000	25,000	12,500
Migrants in Western Europe								
Community of Agape, Italy, Migrant Seminar (Comunità d'Agape—Centro Ecumenico)	—	—	2,500	—	—	—	—	—
Migrant Workers Co-ordinating Committee (Paris)	—	—	—	5,000	—	—	—	—
Total Europe	23,000	10,000	18,000	40,000	72,000	103,500	92,500	87,500
GRAND TOTAL	200,000	200,000	194,000	450,000	500,000	560,045	525,000	434,500

APPENDIX G

Grants to Groups Combating Racism: Facts and Rationale
A Statement by the World Council of Churches, 1978

This explanation of grants made in the Program to Combat Racism was issued by the Council's New York office in August 1978, when the Council announced its grant of $85,000 to the Rhodesian Patriotic Front.

I. WHAT LAY BEHIND THE DECISION

From its beginnings, the modern ecumenical movement has been committed to do battle with racial injustice. In 1924, two dozen years before the founding of the World Council, J. H. Oldham, Secretary of the International Missionary Council (a WCC predecessor organization), wrote a powerful book about racism. In it he said:

> When Christians find in the world a state of things that is not in accord with the truth which they have learned from Christ, their concern is not that it should be explained but that it should be ended. In that temper we must approach everything in the relations between races that cannot be reconciled with the Christian ideal.

1954. Evanston Assembly. The Second Assembly of the World Council expressed the conviction that "any form of segregation based on race, color or ethnic origin is contrary to the Gospel" and called on its member churches to work for the abolition of segregation and discrimination "within their own life and within society."

1965. Central Committee. Through its policy making Central Committee, the WCC supported an appeal "for funds for the legal defense of the victims of unjust accusation and discriminatory laws in South Africa and Rhodesia and aid for them and their dependents." (The only difference between this action and the 1970 action is that in 1965 most of the legal aid funds went to liberal white organizations and now it is going directly to the organizations of the black victims themselves.)

1966. Geneva Conference on Church and Society. This gathering, convened by

97

the World Council, said: "It is not enough for churches and groups to condemn the sin of racial arrogance and oppression. The struggle for radical change in structures will inevitably bring suffering and will demand costly and bitter engagement."

1968. Uppsala Assembly. The Fourth Assembly of the WCC unflinchingly identified the racism practiced by the white skinned against their darker skinned brothers as one of the world's basic problems and a blatant denial of the Christian faith. Uppsala instructed the Council to set up a program to combat racism. It called for a concentration on *white* racism deliberately:

> By focussing on white racism, we are not unaware of other forms of ethnocentrism which produce inter-ethnic and inter-tribal tensions and conflicts throughout the world today. We believe, however, that white racism has special historical significance because its roots lie in powerful, highly developed countries, the stability of which is crucial to any hope for international peace and development.

1969. Notting Hill, London. The Central Committee of the WCC authorized a consultation on racism, which convened at Notting Hill in May of 1969 under the chairmanship of Senator George McGovern of the United States. Several findings and recommendations emerged. These were transmitted to the Central Committee at its meeting the following August.

1969. Central Committee, Canterbury. The Central Committee voted to establish a Program to Combat Racism, to be directed by an International Advisory Committee. The program was to include many elements, including action-oriented research, information, mobilization of member churches, and direct aid to racially oppressed groups. The Central Committee called for creation of a special fund of $500,000 which would be used to make grants to "organizations of oppressed racial groups or organizations supporting victims of racial injustice whose purposes are not inconsonant with the general purposes of the World Council and . . . to be used in their struggle for economic, social and political justice."

II. ALLOCATION OF GRANTS

On September 3, 1970, the Executive Committee of the World Council of Churches announced that $200,000 in WCC funds would be disbursed to nineteen organizations struggling for racial justice in various parts of the world. Almost immediately, questions were raised about the purpose of the grants, the character of the recipient groups, and the long term effect of the action upon the World Council and its member churches. This document is prepared as an attempt to respond to many of the questions which are being raised.

The Director, Dr. Baldwin Sjollema, for the Council's racism unit was employed in February of 1970, and the International Advisory Committee had its first meeting in May. It developed criteria and recommendations concerning the organizations to which the first $200,000 of the special fund should be distributed.

On September 9, 1971, the World Council of Churches allocated a second grant of $200,000 for humanitarian purposes such as legal aid, social, health and educational services to seventeen organizations of oppressed racial groups that are actively engaged in combating white racism.

The Executive Committee of the World Council of Churches, meeting in Bangalore, India in January 1973, made a third set of allocations totalling $200,000 to twenty-five organizations on five continents combating racism.

The Executive Committee of the World Council, meeting in Bad Saarow in the German Democratic Republic, February 1974 approved the distribution of $450,000 to twenty-nine organizations on all six continents. This record sum was made possible by special contributions from churches and individuals supplemented by donations from the governments of Netherlands, Sweden and Norway.

The fifth set of grants was made by the Executive Committee meeting in Geneva, April 1975. A record sum of $479,000 was allocated to twenty-seven organizations of racially oppressed people on six continents. The fund was made possible by donations from individuals, churches and groups, as well as grants from the governments of Netherlands, Sweden and Norway.

Grants totalling $560,000 were approved by the Executive Committee and the Central Committee in August 1976. A total of thirty-seven groups in nineteen countries received assistance in the sixth allocation since the Special Fund was created. The Special Fund derives its income primarily from gifts of local churches and individuals.

In 1977 a total of $530,000 from PCR Special Fund was distributed to thirty-five groups. This amount was approved by the twenty-six member Executive Committee of the World Council of Churches meeting in conjunction with the larger Central Committee in Geneva, Switzerland.

III. THE REACTIONS

Negative reactions have come primarily from white dominated southern Africa and Great Britain. A member of Rhodesia's government, D. Fawcett Phillips, said the World Council should be renamed "Murder Incorporated." The Prime Minister of South Africa, John Vorster, called the action a decision to support "Communist organizations and terrorists." He said that South African churches which are members of the World Council must withdraw or "action would be taken against them."

Sections of the press in Europe and southern Africa have repeated terms like "Communist," "terrorist" and "guerrilla" in describing the recipient groups. Whites outside of Southern Africa have consequently picked up some of the labels and arguments used by white African politicians, whose reactions of rage were predictable.

But from the initiation of the anti-racism program, the World Council has insisted that *no support be given to violence*, even when many Christians were prepared to justify it as a last resort and in the face of the violence perpetuated daily by tyrannical, minority governments in Southern Africa.

The groups applying for grants all agreed to use the funds only for non-military purposes; that is, in social, medical, educational and general relief activity.

Further, grants do not equal unqualified endorsement of every tactic used by a recipient organization, just as traditional relief activities among the victims of the

Nigerial civil war or the Southeast Asia conflict do not imply approval of the politics or strategy of any of the parties involved.

The grants *do* represent general support from the WCC for the long term goals toward which the organizations are working. This, more than the relatively small amounts of money involved, is the chief significance of the action.

IV. SOME CONCLUSIONS

It is clear that there will be some negative consequences of the action. The Executive Committee foresaw this, as did the Central Committee in August of 1969.

The WCC could lose some member churches, which would so some damage to the over-all goal of keeping the world's Christians in communication with one another. But churches are joining and leaving the Council right along. In 1960, three Dutch Reformed churches in South Africa left the WCC following a simple verbal denunciation of apartheid as inconsistent with the Christian faith. The WCC might also lose financial support from some sources, at a time when staff is being trimmed. Finally, the action may cause difficulty, perhaps even physical suffering, for some among the WCC's constituency in certain lands.

On the positive side, four likely results can be seen. As outlined by David Gill of the WCC staff they are:

1. It is a concrete action offering moral support to those engaged in the struggle for racial justice. It helps to counter in a small way the churches' long record of participation, actively or by silence, in the violence of the status quo maintained by white establishments throughout the world for centuries. Said the *Christian Century* in an editorial: "The greatest violence imaginable lurks around that turn of history when non-whites decide that there is no justice or compassion or reason left in the white world."

2. The ecumenical debate about Christian responsibility in the modern world is now out of the ivory tower of calm, academic discussion and thrown open to a much wider constituency, both church and general. WCC staff might have done studies "until they were blue in the face and churned out well balanced documents until their duplication machines froze over, yet never have achieved the breadth of concerned debate which this single action has brought about." (David Gill)

3. The decision is a sign of hope for those who have become increasingly skeptical about the ability of churches to make any real contribution to the building of a more humane world. It is a sign that even the leaders of the church institutions are still able to remember and practice the example of Jesus Christ, who said he came to identify with the poor, the oppressed, the powerless, the alienated—and who asked his followers to go and do likewise.

4. The action is an indication that the WCC is becoming truly a *world* body. No longer is the world Christian community controlled by the thinking and programs of the white churches in the affluent nations. No longer does the WCC take its clues only from its constituents in the privileged lands of the north.

Finally, to return to the situation of the churches in South Africa and Rhodesia, there are signs that the controversy by the WCC action is strengthening the

Council's members there in their determination to resist control by the governments. The Presbyterian Church in South Africa, considered one of the most conservative English language churches in the country, and from the same confessional tradition as the Afrikaans speaking Reformed churches which left WCC a decade ago, voted to stay in the WCC. The vote was close (75 to 57), but the words used in replying to Mr. Vorster's threat were surprisingly blunt:

> The General Assembly of the Presbyterian Church reminds the Prime Minister that its only lord and master is Jesus Christ and it may not serve other masters, and that its task is not necessarily to support the government in power but to be faithful to the Gospel.

Not one of the nine member churches in South Africa has yet withdrawn from the Council. The first response of the South African church leaders was to disassociate themselves from the WCC action but to announce their intention of remaining in the Council. While lamenting the WCC grants, several churchmen also denounced the evils of the apartheid system.

An official of the Methodist Church of South Africa criticized "the majority of white South Africans" for "implicitly supporting . . . daily acts of violence against human dignity carried out . . . in the name of apartheid." The Anglican Bishop of Port Elizabeth in South Africa said: "This unhappy aspect of the Council's work was occasioned by its despair over our failure to deal with the suppression of people here. I do not agree with the Council's decision, but I can understand the motivation born of despair."

It is true that the World Council's action has some risks attached to it. It is even conceivable that history will judge it to have been a mistake. But at this moment, responsible, cautious, elected representatives of much of world Christianity see the imperative in other terms. No longer is silence or even the right words an adequate response. As Miss Webb and Dr. Payne said in their letter to the *London Times*:

> For the churches of the world piety is not enough. The program to combat racism aims at helping forward efforts to secure basic human rights and to do so within certain agreed and well defined guidelines. It is those who do nothing or are content with words only, who can rightly be described as "pessimistic."

The WCC Program to Combat Racism

A Statement by the Presbyterian Church in Ireland, 1978

The Presbyterian Church in Ireland was one of the three denominations that suspended their membership in the World Council of Churches in protest against the $85,000 grant made by the Program to Combat Racism to the Rhodesian Patriotic Front in August 1978. Below are the resolution and statement issued in September 1978 by the Inter-Church Relations Board of the Presbyterian Church in Ireland. The text is from Conflict Studies No. 105 *(London: Institute for the Study of Conflict, March 1979).*

RESOLUTION

We affirm that Racism of any colour, is an offence against God the Father, Creator of us all, against the universal Gospel of His Son our Saviour, Jesus Christ, and against the communion of the Holy Spirit. It is both cause and excuse for great evils in the world in which, like so many others, we have had a part; and of hidden temptations even yet often masked behind self-righteous protestations.

The World Council of Churches' concern to combat Racism is, in principle, thoroughly justified: and all Christians should be committed to the cause, both in their own society and throughout the world. Yet the operation of the Council's particular "Programme to Combat Racism" and especially of the associated "Special Fund" is open to serious criticism for genuine Christian reasons. The Inter-Church Relations Board therefore urges the World Council of Churches to make a thorough reappraisal of the Special Fund of the Programme to Combat Racism and its administration.

The accompanying Statement on the World Council of Churches Programme to Combat Racism and the Special Fund is received and commended for careful consideration both by members of our own Church and the responsible committees and officers of the World Council of Churches.

The Very Rev. Dr. A. J. Weir, Rev. Douglas Armstrong, Rev. W. M. Craig, Rev.

K. N. E. Newell, Mr. Robert Ferguson and Mr. W. J. McWilliam are appointed as a delegation to visit representatives of the World Council of Churches and to urge upon them the deep concern felt in our Church particularly over the issues raised by the Special Fund of the Programme to Combat Racism especially following the recent grant of 85,000 dollars from the Special Fund to the Patriotic Front of Zimbabwe and the insensitivity of its timing.

STATEMENT

PART 1. General Considerations

1. From the outset, our Presbyterian Church in Ireland and Inter-Church Relations Board have submitted criticisms of the policies adopted by the World Council of Churches' "Programme to Combat Racism" and the associated "Special Fund" as well as trying to explain these to our members—cf. our General Assembly Reports: 1971, pp. 70-72; 1972, p. 89 and 1975, pp. 74-85. We, accordingly, were among those Churches which protested at the use for grants of funds taken from the WCC Reserve Account, which had not been subscribed for this purpose; and we have continued from conviction to refuse to contribute to the "Special Fund" which was set up subsequently and from which grants to "Anti-Racist" organisations have been made.

That the administration costs of this "Special Fund" should still be borne, it would appear, by the WCC generally, no matter how marginal relatively the amounts involved, does not give confidence in the organisation's treatment of those different views.

2. To make payments without provision for accountability, such as we would apply strictly to ourselves and seek in all our sister Churches, when these happen to be grants to "Anti-Racist" organisations appears simply as an example of Racism in reverse. It may be pleasing to the recipients and their friends, but can only help to confirm doubts and prejudices for others in the Church and in society generally. The reactions are the stronger when the grants are made to organisations actively pursuing political power and military objectives, however earmarked the particular contributions may be for "humanitarian work." We urge that account should be taken of lessons learnt from our own tragic and bitter experience in Ireland during these past years.

3. The policies which have been followed, together with the manner of their presentation and the publicity they have received, have not only coloured the character of the Special Fund but also affected the general Programme to Combat Racism. All too many have been led to interpret the aim as being more one of "solidarity with conflict and terrorism" rather than "solidarity with sufferers from injustice." Indeed, there is an increasing sense, which seems not to be confined to our Church or land, that the evangelical and Christian character professed by the WCC is itself being gravely compromised. In all humbleness before God, we therefore call on those who bear either personal or collective responsibility for these operations, urgently, prayerfully and radically to reconsider their Programme and the use of the Special Fund.

PART II. Particular Considerations (urged in the light of Church experience in our Irish situation)

4. Concern expressed by Christians in other lands for a troubled suffering community, is a precious thing when it is guided by understanding and practical co-operation which does not ignore or by-pass the local Churches. It does an ecumenical injury so to by-pass them: and it demonstrates a kind of new colonialism when particular partisan organisations are supported on the selection of outsiders, who may be ill-informed or deliberately misinformed.

5. Grants made by well-intentioned donors to paramilitary or guerrilla groups, or to their supporting organisations, do not end simply with humanitarian aid, even when so used, but strengthen generally the power of the particular group or individual administering them. Church support for humanitarian work in such situations where there is great personal or social need, should be through independent and, preferably, Church-related agencies. This policy, for instance, which is being followed for Church aid within Rhodesia/Zimbabwe, should be applied as much to territories outside. It would be as wrong and offensive to entrust ecumenical Church grants, however earmarked, to the organisations of Ian Smith and his colleagues as it is to the Patriotic Front in their violent confrontation.

6. Though Christian citizens, of any race, time and again may have felt themselves compelled to go to war for self-defence or liberation from injustice, we recognise increasingly that Christian Churches should exercise caution and restraint in the ways in which they lend support to such an awful and ambiguous course. Misdirected actions by Churches in the past are grounds for repentance, but not justification for their repetition to give a kind of "balance" in wrongdoing that leads only to an interminable chain reaction. The sufferings and atrocities that all wars unleash upon the innocent are compounded in terrorist operations which lack any framework of public accountability and law. Propaganda arguments over responsibility for particular atrocities do not change the real situation of violence being faced.

7. In wars and civil conflicts, potential or actual, Christians are to be found not only upon one side. Churches which may seek so to align them and dictate their votes or personal allegiances, whether at the behest of particular enthusiasts or of ecclesiastical and ecumenical establishments, have been generally repudiated both by history and experience. In the event, the "holy cause" has too often led to an unholy situation and the "liberators" to a new enslavement. This, that we have faced, we believe also applies to the terrible prospect of racial "civil war" in the family of mankind.

8. Christians, indeed, must each make his or her own political choice of one kind or another. Christian leaders, Churches and Church organisations for their part should rightly seek to bring the light of God's Word and the leading of the Holy Spirit to bear upon the issues facing men and women in the world; but such testimony should stop short of trying to impose a corporate commitment to one political grouping, whether in government, opposition or revolt, even when there may be general sympathy for their aims. This should be doubly so for Churches and Church organisations which are not composed of citizens of the State concerned. Religion, we well know, may too easily be made the tool of politics and politicians, old or new nationally or internationally—and Churches tools likewise.

APPENDIX I

Program to Combat Racism
A Statement by the WCC Central Committee, 1979

This statement (Document No. 44A, Revised) was approved by the Central Committee of the World Council of Churches, meeting in Kingston, Jamaica, on January 10, 1979.

1. *Comments on PCR Report*

   The Unit Report on PCR (Central Committee document no. 2) was *received.* In the ensuing discussion there was unanimous agreement that well-financed propaganda agencies in the media, hostile to PCR and the WCC in general, were distorting the member churches' understanding of PCR's work. Mention was made in particular of the recent scandal in South Africa which exposed the clandestine efforts of the South African Government to influence news agencies in the Western world.

   We were concerned that member churches should be helped to question the sources of information about PCR's activities and to examine press reports with critical judgment; for example, information issued by racist government agencies or censored by them, as well as by private organisations and published in religious and secular press. Attention should be given to terminology such as "execution," "assassination," "guerrilla," "terrorist," etc. Also, in our own dissemination of information, the very diverse activities of PCR which are not limited to Southern Africa or the Special Fund, should be given greater prominence.

   We were also of the view that although the adverse image and understanding of PCR needs to be changed, the purpose and thrust of PCR itself *are still valid.* We are hopeful that with member churches alerted to the areas of distortion and misinterpretation, even greater support for PCR and the Special Fund would be forthcoming. However we noted that wherever the opportunity to rebut false allegations about PCR was seized in public debate, a better informed constituency was usually the result.

   We were conscious of the special difficulties encountered by some churches and Christians in countries with strong kinship, investment and other economic ties with racist societies in Southern Africa, in supporting or even voicing support of programmes of solidarity with racially oppressed people in those societies. We note also those questions and criticisms voiced in good faith by some member churches. At the same time we remain sensitive to the witness of churches and Christians within Southern Africa and express our solidarity with all those who are banned and detained, and assure them of our prayers.

The General Secretary's recommendation for a process of consultation on combating racism in the 80's was strongly welcomed, since there are continuing perplexities in some churches over PCR and the Special Fund.

Recommendations

It is accordingly recommended that:
i) The Central Committee endorses the view of the Review Committee that the administration of the Special Fund "has so far been in accordance with the established and accepted criteria set by the Central Committee," and that the PCR should be encouraged to continue its work in situations of racial discrimination in the world today and that the Special Fund be continued with clearer interpretation to increase comprehension in the churches.
ii) The Central Committee further resolves, in the light of changing circumstances and escalation of racism, to accept the proposal of the General Secretary that a process of consultation, to be set in motion as soon as possible, on how the churches may be involved in combating racism in the 1980's be given priority. In doing this, account should be taken of the experience gained, the questions raised and the criticisms made during the ten years of existence of this programme.

The process of consultation should include meetings having a balanced representation and involving:
    a) representatives of the member churches,
    b) representatives of race relations' desks of member churches, national and regional councils,
    c) representatives of the racially oppressed.

This process should include a major consultation whose recommendations and deliberations should be made available to the Central Committee in 1980.

Since many of the questions and criticisms raised are to be found in Central Committee document No. 17: Background Paper on Southern Africa, particularly Part III entitled "Issues and Dilemmas in the Present Debate," and Unit II Committee document 12E containing an evaluation of the background paper "South Africa's Hope—What Price Now?" these papers among others should form a basis for consultation and discussion as suggested above, without restricting them to the Southern Africa situation.
iii) The financial implications of this process of consultation should be considered by the Finance Committee at the Central Committee.
iv) The General Secretary should be requested to report to the Executive Committee in September 1979 on the progress made.

2. *Investments, Trade and Bank Loans to South Africa*
The Central Committee reaffirms its request to PCR to give special attention to the issues of investments and trade (Central Committee Utrecht 1972), bank loans (Central Committee West Berlin 1974) to South Africa at this time when

foreign economic interests stand out as a major factor favoring the maintenance and strengthening of Apartheid, and also when several member churches and church groups are becoming increasingly involved in campaigns against investments in South Africa and boycott the consumer goods from that country. Central Committee therefore urges renewed PCR concentration on these issues.

3. *Organized White Mass Migration from Southern Africa*
Oppressed racial groups and churches continue to express concern about the organized white mass migration from Southern Africa to a number of countries in North and Latin America, Western Europe, Australia and New Zealand.
   In 1977 the Central Committee recommended to the member churches the following actions:
   —"to express grave concern at the explosive implications of the reported scheme of the Bolivian Government to receive white settlers en masse from Southern Africa to Latin America, recognizing that this would constitute a threat to the indigenous people of the Latin American continent;
   —to call attention to the fact that any mass migration of white settlers from Southern Africa would simply encourage the transfer of racism to another society."
It is therefore recommended that: PCR in cooperation with other sub-units including the Migration Secretariat should intensify its investigation into, and action on, the issue of organized white mass migration from Southern Africa especially into those countries with racially oppressed peoples.

4. *Racism in Children's and School Text Books*
The Unit Committee strongly commends the PCR's efforts to combat racism in children's and school text books as well as in christian educational material. The report and study guide of a first regional workshop should be sent to all member churches and national and regional councils for their consideration and action.

5. *Racism in Asia*
The Central Committee in 1976 requested PCR to give major attention to racism in Asia as of 1979. In 1977, the Central Committee recommended that "regional ecumenical bodies be involved in the development of PCR's agenda."
In pursuance of this recommendation a workshop was held in Auckland, New Zealand, 1978 on "Race and Minority issues in Asia," sponsored by WCC/PCR and CCA/Urban Rural Mission (Unit Doc. 12).
   The workshop gathered 45 people from 12 countries and dealt with a wide variety of issues, including minority rights, race, identity, national unity, justice and participation. The Workshop made recommendations (Unit Doc. 12c, p. 6) and urged the churches to stand in solidarity with racially oppressed minorities in Asia.
   The Central Committee requests PCR to continue to work with CCA/URM and member churches in the area on race and minority issues, including:

a) collection and publication of testimonies on land and life experience in the struggle for justice;
b) production and distribution of audio-visual aid material for educational purposes;
c) sponsoring of further workshops and training possibilities to improve the organizational capability of racially oppressed minorities.

6. *Landrights and Racially Oppressed Indigenous People*

i) The Central Committee receives the document on "Landrights and racially oppressed indigenous peoples" (Unit Committee document no. 12b) with particular emphasis on the situations in Australia and Brazil, as the first result of PCR's research for action programs in this area. It requests that information on the issue be made available to the member churches and that further cooperation be worked out with the churches in Australia and Brazil.

ii) The Central Committee requests the PCR to indicate a plan of action together with all the churches in Australia and Brazil, and particularly with organizations of the racially oppressed and support groups in these countries. This plan of action should promote further research and plans of action in these countries.

iii) The Central Committee requests that serious attention be given to adequate staffing for this next state of the program.

Notes

Chapter One

1. *Report of the Freedom House Mission to Observe the Common Roll Election in Zimbabwe Rhodesia: April 1979* (New York: Freedom House, 1979), p. 5.
2. "Going 'Beyond Charity,' " *Time*, October 2, 1978, p. 46.
3. Stephen Chapman, "Killing for Christ," *The New Republic*, October 21, 1978, p. 8.
4. Resolution adopted September 29, 1978. Reprinted in George Austin, *World Council of Churches' Programme to Combat Racism*, Conflict Studies No. 105 (London: Institute for the Study of Conflict, March 1979), pp. 19, 20.
5. Quoted in Chapman, "Killing for Christ," p. 7.
6. Edward Norman, *Christianity and the World Order* (New York: Oxford University Press, 1979), p. 81.
7. This conforms to the definition in Charles Wolf, Jr., *United States Policy in the Third World* (Boston: Little, Brown & Co., 1967), pp. vii, viii.
8. Paul Ramsey, *Who Speaks for the Church?* (Nashville: Abingdon Press, 1967). See also Ernest W. Lefever, "Evanston and International Affairs," *Christianity and Crisis*, November 29, 1954.

Chapter Two

1. *Findings and Decisions, First Assembly of the World Council of Churches* (Geneva: World Council of Churches, 1948), p. 8.
2. W. A. Visser 't Hooft, ed., *The First Assembly of the World Council of Churches* (New York: Harper & Brothers, 1949), p. 76.
3. Ibid., p. 80.
4. *The Ten Formative Years 1938-1948* (Geneva: World Council of Churches, 1948), p. 9.
5. W. A. Visser 't Hooft, ed., *The Evanston Report* (New York: Harper & Brothers, 1955), p. 113.
6. W. A. Visser 't Hooft, "World Conference on Church and Society," *The Ecumenical Review*, October 1966, p. 421.
7. Ibid., p. 423.
8. M. M. Thomas, "The Situation in Asia—II," *Man's Disorder and God's Design* (New York: Harper & Brothers, 1949), 3:71.
9. Visser 't Hooft, *The First Assembly*, p. 79.
10. Ibid., p. 91.
11. Ibid., p. 75.
12. Paul Bock, *In Search of a Responsible World Society* (Philadelphia: Westminster Press, 1974), p. 137.
13. Visser 't Hooft, *The Evanston Report*, p. 133.

14. Ernest W. Lefever, "Evanston on International Affairs," *Christianity and Crisis*, November 29, 1954, p. 159.

15. Visser 't Hooft, *The Evanston Report*, p. 147.

16. Ibid., p. 137.

17. Ibid., p. 126.

18. Ibid., p. 147.

19. Ibid., pp. 147, 148.

20. Ibid., p. 116.

21. Ibid., p. 155.

22. *Evanston to New Delhi* (Geneva: World Council of Churches, 1961), p. 49.

23. Paul Abrecht, "The Development of Ecumenical Social Thought and Action," in *A History of the Ecumenical Movement, Volume II, 1948-1968*, ed. Harold E. Fey (Philadelphia: Westminster Press, 1970), p. 250.

24. John Marcum, *The Angolan Revolution: The Anatomy of an Explosion (1950-1962)* (Cambridge, Mass.: The M.I.T. Press, 1969), pp. 135-80.

25. W. A. Visser 't Hooft, ed., *The New Delhi Report* (New York: Association Press, 1962), p. 101.

26. Ibid., p. 100.

27. Ibid., pp. 275, 276.

Chapter Three

1. Edward Norman, *Christianity and the World Order* (New York: Oxford University Press, 1979), p. 6.

2. Roger Mehl, writing in *Le Monde*, July 27, 1966; quoted by Paul Abrecht, "The Development of Ecumenical Social Thought and Action," in *A History of the Ecumenical Movement, Volume II, 1948-1968*, ed. Harold E. Fey (Philadelphia: Westminster Press, 1970), p. 255.

3. Richard John Neuhaus, "Toeing the Line at the Cutting Edge," *Worldview*, June 1977, p. 18.

4. Quoted in Ernest W. Lefever, "Church and Politics: The Protestant Debate," *The Reporter*, January 11, 1968, p. 40.

5. Ibid.

6. *Official Report: World Conference on Church and Society* (Geneva: World Council of Churches, 1967), p. 10.

7. Paul Bock, *In Search of a Responsible Society* (Philadelphia: Westminster Press, 1974), p. 147.

8. *Official Report*, p. 17.

9. Ibid., p. 18.

10. Ibid., p. 99.

11. Ibid., p. 106.

12. Ibid., p. 143.

13. Jacques Ellul, "Mirror of These Ten Years," *The Christian Century*, February 18, 1970, p. 202.

14. Paul Ramsey, *Who Speaks for the Church?* (Nashville: Abingdon Press, 1967).

15. *Official Report*, p. 147.

16. Norman Goodall, ed., *The Uppsala Report* (Geneva: World Council of Churches, 1968), p. 48.

17. *Uppsala to Nairobi* (New York: Friendship Press, 1975), p. 147.

Chapter Four

1. Edward Norman, *Christianity and the World Order* (New York: Oxford University Press, 1979), p. 59.

2. Senate Committee Report, *Departments of State, Justice, and Commerce, The Judiciary, and Related Agencies Appropriations Bill, 1979*, July 28, 1978.

3. Harry Genet, "World Council of Churches: A Case of Indigestion," *Christianity Today*, February 2, 1979, p. 52.

4. Ibid., p. 53.

5. Document No. 44A (Revised), World Council of Churches Central Committee, January 10, 1979; all quotations in this paragraph and the next one are from this report.

6. Quoted in "Going 'Beyond Charity,'" *Time*, October 2, 1978, p. 46.

7. Jean Chaffey Lyles, "That $85,000 Grant," *The Christian Century*, September 20, 1978, p. 844.

8. "Violence, Nonviolence and the Struggle for Social Justice," *The Ecumenical Review*, October 1973, p. 443.

9. Ibid., p. 442.

10. David M. Paton, ed., *Breaking Barriers: Nairobi 1975* (Grand Rapids: William B. Eerdmans, 1976), p. 100.

11. Ibid.

12. *Uppsala to Nairobi* (New York: Friendship Press, 1975), p. 80.

13. For a summary see Paton, *Breaking Barriers*, pp. 12-14.

14. Richard John Neuhaus, "Toeing the Line at the Cutting Edge," *Worldview*, June 1977, p. 18.

15. *Uppsala to Nairobi*, p. 192.

16. Peter L. Berger, *Pyramids of Sacrifice* (New York: Basic Books, 1974), p. 113.

17. Orthodox Theological Society of America, "Orthodox Christian Reflections on the Documentation for the World Council of Churches' Fifth Assembly," May 30, 1975.

18. Ibid.

19. Paton, *Breaking Barriers*, p. 131.

20. Norman, *Christianity and the World Order*, p. 60.

21. Paton, *Breaking Barriers*, p. 23. The "black messiahs" remark was an ad lib (Paul G. Schrotenboer to Ernest W. Lefever, December 21, 1978).

22. See Benjamin E. Mays, comp., *A Gospel for the Social Awakening: Selections From the Writings of Walter Rauschenbusch* (New York: Association Press, 1950).

23. Paton, *Breaking Barriers*, p. 103.

24. Ibid., p. 111.

25. Ibid., p. 174.

26. Ibid.

27. Ibid., p. 81.

28. Ibid., p. 131.
29. *One World*, March 1978, p. 11.

Chapter Five

1. Edward Norman, *Christianity and the World Order* (New York: Oxford University Press, 1979), p. 12.
2. Daniel Patrick Moynihan, "The United States in Opposition," *Commentary*, March 1975 (reprinted by the Ethics and Public Policy Center).
3. Peter L. Berger, *Facing Up to Modernity: Excursions in Society, Politics, and Religion* (New York: Basic Books, 1977), esp. pp. 145-94. Also "Ethics and the Present Class Struggle," *Worldview*, April 1978 (reprinted by the Ethics and Public Policy Center as *Ethics and the New Class*).
4. Richard John Neuhaus, "Toeing the Line at the Cutting Edge," *Worldview*, June 1977 (reprinted by the Ethics and Public Policy Center as *The World Council of Churches and Radical Chic*).
5. P. T. Bauer, "Western Guilt and Third World Poverty," *Commentary*, January 1976 (reprinted by the Ethics and Public Policy Center).
6. Quoted in Norman, *Christianity and the World Order*, p. 11.
7. Ibid., p. 15.
8. Ibid.
9. Quoted in ibid., p. 26.
10. Neuhaus, "Toeing the Line," p. 22.
11. Norman, *Christianity and the World Order*, pp. 23, 24. See also p. 5.
12. *Gaudium et Spes: Pastoral Constitution on the Church and the World of Today* (London: Catholic Truth Society, 1966), p. 79.
13. Quoted in Donald Read, *Cobden and Bright: A Victorian Political Partnership* (London: E. Arnold, 1967), p. 65.
14. Quoted in Walter W. VanKirk, *Religion Renounces War* (Chicago: Willett, Clark and Co., 1934), p. 262.
15. Quoted on B.B.C. Radio 4, "Sunday," November 6, 1977.
16. Quoted in Norman, *Christianity and the World Order*, pp. 22, 23.
17. This point was made by Cynthia Wedel, an American who was then one of the six WCC presidents, in an interview with the author on August 17, 1978.
18. Quoted in "WCC: An Uncertain Sound?," *Christianity Today*, February 16, 1979, p. 12.
19. Quoted in Ernest W. Lefever, "Church and Politics: The Protestant Debate," *The Reporter*, January 11, 1968, p. 42.
20. Ibid.
21. Quoted in "WCC: An Uncertain Sound?," p. 12.
22. Ibid. See also Neuhaus, "Toeing the Line," p. 16.
23. Paul Ramsey, *Who Speaks for the Church?* (Nashville: Abingdon Press, 1967), pp. 15, 16.
24. Neuhaus, "Toeing the Line," p. 18.

Index of Persons and Countries